Developing
High Performance
Tennis Players

D1319465

Edgar Giffenig

M. Ed. (Exercise Physiology), National Coach
in the U.S., Germany and Mexico

Table of Contents

PART I
Introduction

PART II
Developing Better Weapons for Battle

PART III
Teaching How to Use These Weapons

Part IV

Optimizing your Players' Games to Achieve Consistent Performances

Part V

Putting it all Together

Part VI

Reference Library

Acknowledgements

EG's COACHING WEAPONS

Throughout the book, this icon will be used to highlight statements which the author deemed specially relevant or noteworthy.

SUMMARY & CONCLUSIONS

The summary and conclusions icon indicates sections where the author has condensed information and drawn conclusions.

Acknowledgements

In summarizing 40 years on the court, it is very difficult to acknowledge everyone who has positively influenced me during that time. I should probably start by thanking my family, since they were the ones who introduced me to this wonderful sport: my mother Pilar and my dad Edgar, who spent a great deal of time and energy supporting me and my tennis economically and emotionally, my grandfather Angel, who always played with me when I slept over and my grandmothers Maria and Käthe, who always enjoyed watching me play. Later on of course, my wife Lyndell deserves my gratitude for putting up with the demands of high performance coaching, including the frequent moves from city to city and country to country following better coaching opportunities, and for her willingness to host and take care of young tennis players who continually dart in and out of our lives.

I also should thank my daughters Pilar, Lyndell and Katya, for allowing me to spend time with them on the court teaching them to play but also learning a great deal from them.

Growing up, I was fortunate enough to make many good friends while playing and competing. I have many fond memories of the time I spent at the Junior Club in Mexico City and later on in Austin, Texas, as a member of the Tennis Team at the University of Texas. Many thanks to all my practice partners, opponents and teammates who helped me hone my skills; too many to list.

Many superb coaches contributed to my understanding of the game, and it would be impossible to acknowledge all of them. However, I was lucky enough to spend a considerable time with some of them: George Toley, Dave Snyder, Jeff Moore, Nick Saviano, Stan Smith, Rodney Harmon, John Benson, Carol Watson, José Higueras, Bobby Bernstein, Alan Ma, Scott Del Mastro, Paul Sindhunatha, Peter Born, Zdenek Zofka, Peter Pfannkoch, Miguel Angel Reyes Varela and Guillermo Stevens. Thank you for your friendship and insight into the game. I would also like to express my gratitude to everyone who allowed me to instruct them, since many of my students were also my best teachers. I wish to recognize my good friends: John Posey, for his editing advice; John Gruen, for his beautiful pictures; and especially, Edward Letteron, who spent many hours helping me put this book together.

Finally, I would like to thank my friends at TennisGate, Oliver Heuft and Jürgen Müller, for inviting me to join their great project. Our similar coaching philosophy and enthusiasm for the game makes for a great partnership.

Keep your Cup Half Empty

"Keep your Cup Half Empty"; several years ago I came across this saying, which I always try to keep in mind.

Throughout our lives, we form our ideas about the world based on our experiences, and these ideas become our truths, our interpretation of the world. They define what we believe is right and wrong, good and bad, healthy and unhealthy, etc. Once we adopt these truths we fight ferociously to hold on to them. We become their champions and unconsciously seek out opportunities to validate them.

If, for example, we believe that people in large cities are rude, every time we are in a large city, our minds will zero in on any rude action around us and dismiss all acts of kindness. If we are looking to buy the newest Wilson racquet, suddenly we start seeing that racquet everywhere. We become aware of all new Wilson racquets we previously never noticed.

We often experience this phenomenon as coaches when talking to our students about a match. The game we saw from the outside seems totally different from the one our student experienced. A student with a weak backhand will say: "I lost because I missed every backhand" when he really missed more forehands. He remembers the backhand errors because they follow and confirm his preconceptions.

This is human nature. Looking back over my career, it is amazing to recognize how many times I finally realized that a concept that sounded ridiculous at the time and that went against everything I had learned ended up becoming my new "truth" later on. And similarly, many concepts that I fiercely defended ended up not being as infallible as I thought.

Be open to new ideas. "Keep your Cup Half Empty." You cannot add to a full cup. Do not dismiss novel concepts just because they do not fit into your neatly kept mental tennis drawer. Give new ideas a chance. Analyze them objectively, and try them out. You may be pleasantly surprised with the result.

PART I

Introduction

You will learn about my coaching philosophy as well as the basic structure for the player development system I propose.

PREFACE AND INTRODUCTION

Preface

Tennis has been part of my life since I was born. My earliest memories of the game have me building clay cakes on the side of the court while my mother played. My grandfather played Davis Cup for Mexico, and my grandmother was the top player in Mexico for seven years. Tennis is in my blood, and I have been passionate about it since I started playing seriously at age nine. Since then, I have been lucky enough to have been involved in competitive tennis for more than 40 years. As a player, I was always ranked among the best juniors in Mexico and represented the country in several international competitions. Eventually, I played for the University of Texas, where I finished a BA degree in business and ME in Exercise Physiology. However, my love of the game pulled me away from the business world and into high performance coaching. I started as assistant coach for the University of Texas, and have spent the last 25 years working with some of the best juniors in the world, as a National Coach for the USTA, the German Federation and the Mexican Federation.

The following book is an attempt to summarize my experience in tennis, both as a player and as a coach. It takes the form of a training system that addresses the intricate and subtle aspects of the game and presents a structured approach to coaching and training the competitive player.

The book starts with an analysis of the game and the elements that determine a player's success. Then it proposes a detailed training plan that tackles all the important aspects involved in developing an elite player.

This program has proven to be very effective in my coaching career. I hope it will help you improve your understanding of this amazing game and will give you some additional tools to become a better coach or player.

It looks so easy!

Introduction

Great tennis players make the game look easy. They seem to play effortlessly and always under control. They are smart, crafty and intelligent, always able to play the right shot at the right time. So, how does a top player achieve this mastery of the game?

Tennis is a complex game that requires the integration of many skills: technique, tactical expertise, physical fitness, and mental dexterity, and great players are able to optimize and combine all of these elements into their games. However, integrating all of these skills is not that easy.

As coaches, we all have biases and based on our background and experiences tend to focus on some skills more than others. In addition, the industry itself tends to go through cycles where coaches are indirectly encouraged to emphasize certain skills over others, and finally, each player is different and changes as he develops, forcing the coach to constantly shift the focus of practice.

Effectively maximizing the potential of our players in every key area is a true balancing act that takes experience, planning, discipline, patience and, most importantly, a well thought out coaching system that addresses all aspects of the game, while providing the necessary flexibility in its implementation.

Here is an example of such a system.

INTEGRATED TRAINING: THE PROGRAM

Many times as coaches we fail to see the whole picture because we are so focused on the details that we truly "can't see the forest for the trees." We tend to get stuck on certain elements and are prone to waste valuable time unless we get into the habit of frequently evaluating what we are doing. From time to time, it is very helpful to step back and remember what the game is all about, in essence: a contact sport without contact, a battle of skills in which a player attacks and defends against an opponent using his strokes as weapons. From this perspective, it is easier to keep our ultimate goals in mind, which basically boil down to this:

As in any other battle, to win one has to accomplish the following:
>> Develop better weapons than the opponent.
>> Know how to use those weapons more effectively than the opponent.
>> Be able to do both of these consistently.

Let's translate this into tennis language:
To win more, every coach needs to help his players achieve the following goals:
>> Develop better strokes.
>> Know how to use these strokes effectively.
>> Be able to perform well and consistently under pressure.

The training model I propose is built around achieving these objectives.

It is important to mention here that although I will address each of these goals separately for the sake of simplicity in my explanation, all these goals should be tackled simultaneously throughout the developmental process.

The idea is not to work first on developing strokes, then on learning how to use these strokes, and finally on performing under pressure. All these skills should be pursued at the same time.

Of course, there are times when one of these aspects has to be emphasized more than the others, but we should always strive for balance in our training. (You will find in-depth information on how to structure your practices in Part V – Putting it all Together.)

Tennis is a battle!

Let's look at our first training goal:

DEVELOP BETTER STROKES THAN THE OPPONENT

Technology has given coaches the opportunity to dissect and analyze professional technique like never before. However, a common mistake that should be avoided is to focus too much on teaching specific movement patterns that should conform to some set guidelines, as opposed to teaching weapons to win a battle. Although certain common elements have to be present in every effective stroke, the focus should never be solely on the form of the stroke but rather on the resulting ball trajectory. This difference, although seemingly trivial, is very significant. Many lessons and practices revolve around teaching six main strokes: forehand, backhand, forehand volley, backhand volley, overhead and serve. The drills and lessons are set up to promote repetition of similar movement patterns to master the perpetually elusive perfect swing. If there is a coach, he will feed the same ball over and over and correct the differences between the form of the student and the picture of the perfect stroke that he has in his mind. Similarly, if two players are practicing, they will use drills in which they hit balls over and over working on achieving their mental image of the perfect stroke.

During a match, however, the important thing is what happens as a result of swinging. More importantly, during match play there are an infinite number of different types of shots that any player has to face. Each incoming shot presents a unique mix of spin, speed, height and direction so a player's real skill is determined by his ability to adjust and respond to all of these different shots in an effective way and not on the form of his stroke. Moreover, every shot a player hits has different goals as well in terms of direction, spin, speed and height. Therefore, the technical objective of any player aspiring to be competitive should be to develop **Stroke Flexibility** – strokes that will allow him to hit any type of shot (any mixture of spin, speed, height and direction) he might need as well as provide him with the ability to handle any type of shot hit to him by the opponent. In other words, total ball control.

So, instead of working on perfecting the forehand or backhand swinging pattern, a player should work on learning to handle any type of shot coming to the forehand side or to the backhand side of his body, as well as being able to respond to each of these shots with the desired combination of speed, spin, and placement.

Let us look at how this can be achieved.

WALK THE TALK!

Tennis is a challenging game with many ups and downs, and its skills only become easy after many years of practice. Sometimes as coaches we get frustrated because we assume our students should be able to perform some skills that seem easy to us, and it is difficult for us to empathize with our struggling players.

We tend to forget very quickly how difficult it is to finish that run when everything is hurting or to push to complete the last series of pushups. Likewise, "Keep the ball in play" is a lot harder when you are the one trying to keep the ball in play.

The best way to get a reality check is to get dirty, to put it on the line. Seek opportunities to drill with your players, condition with them and find matches that will push you as a player.

It is like magic. I always feel much more empathetic after a first-class battle; nothing like a tough practice or tournament to help you regain perspective.

Developing better Weapons for Battle

You will learn about the first important concept of the training system: how to develop stroke flexibility in your players and the technical base to succeed in competition.

DEVELOPING STROKE FLEXIBILITY

From our previous discussion, you know that many technical practices use mostly drills that involve **a high degree of stroke repetition.** This helps develop a more consistent swinging pattern, but not necessarily more effective shots. If one wants to become a great chef, one needs to experiment with a great deal of ingredients and condiments. By cooking burgers every time, one will eventually cook a great burger, but one will definitely not become a chef.

EG's COACHING WEAPONS

Variability is the key to greatness in cooking, tennis and probably anything in life. True mastery can only be achieved through maturity, and maturity is nothing more than an accumulation of a great variety of experiences.

Therefore, to develop more effective shots, the traditional way of training needs to be adjusted to allow players to practice with a much greater degree of variability, forcing the players to constantly adapt and thus develop the desired stroke flexibility.

Even at a beginner's level, the concept of variability should be an integral part of the learning process. Ideally, the coach should teach beginners to rally with each other as soon as possible, avoiding the use of the basket as the main teaching tool. When players learn mostly by hitting balls fed from a basket, they face a huge shock the first time they try to play with someone other than the coach. They realize that it is a lot harder to play tennis when the ball is not fed at an ideal height and speed or that it is very difficult to keep a rally going when your shots go all over the court.

A much better alternative is to learn to play tennis by modifying the length of the court and the type of balls used to help beginners experience the game from the first lesson.

Players will enjoy the game much faster if they are taught a form of real tennis from the first lesson. Real tennis involves great variability and a large degree of control: two players hitting with each other, not one feeding a ball from a basket and the other one hitting it over the net.
By starting the players close to the net and using slower balls (foam or slower balls are readily available), a coach can allow players to experience the feel of the game from the first lesson. As the

It is more fun to learn when you are able to rally immediately.

players improve their ability to rally with slower balls from a short distance to the net, the coach can proceed to lengthen the distance between the players and use other types of balls until the players can comfortably rally from the baseline with regular balls. (In fact, in this respect the teaching industry is slowly changing, and introducing tennis to children and beginners by modifying equipment and courts is much more common.)

Once players can rally comfortably from the baseline, the coach should force the players to constantly adjust, by offering lessons with a high degree of variability. Players should experience hitting the ball at different heights, speeds, spins and directions every time they are on the court. Here are a few drills to help beginners and low intermediate players experience ball control in a whole new light.

1. Different Heights

Players have to hit the ball at three different heights: low, up to four feet over the net; medium, between five and 11 feet over the net; and high, over 12 feet. At first, the players should focus on constantly keeping the ball at a certain height. After they are comfortable doing this, then they should vary their height in the same rally.

2. Different Lengths

Players should experiment with three lengths: short, inside the service box; medium, just past the service line; and long, close to the baseline. One good progression is to start by trying to keep the ball inside the service box, then move back and try to hit the ball as close to the baseline as possible. After a while, players should work on rallying while letting the ball bounce twice to force them to hit the ball short.

Both bounces should land inside the baseline. Finally, players should try to rally hitting very short shots that will bounce three times inside the baseline every time.

3. Different speeds

Players should experiment with three different speeds: slow, medium and fast. The ideal speed will be different for each player, but the idea is to stay under control, even with the fast hits. If players are missing too much, they should adjust their swing speed accordingly.

These are just a few drills to help you understand the concept. Devise your own drills, mixing up all the variables according to your players' ability.

Once the players acquire a certain degree of control the coach should introduce the most important element involved in developing stroke flexibility: spin.

THE MAGIC OF SPIN

Understanding and feeling comfortable with spin is the first large obstacle for beginning and intermediate players, and one most players fail to overcome. Being able to hit with different spins is the main advantage advanced players have over everyone else. Spin opens the door to a whole new world of possibilities, allowing the players to control the ball much better at higher speeds.

There are three types of spins that any aspiring player should master: flat drive, topspin and slice. Every shot in tennis has one of these types of spin to different degrees, and the ability to hit the ball with different types and degrees of spin will provide the groundwork to achieve the necessary ball control to develop as a player.

The following exercise will help the players understand and feel comfortable with the concept of spin.

SPIN DRILLS

Introduction to Spin

There are several ways to introduce spin to your players. Here are a few ideas that have worked for me.

Use a Large Light Ball

Using a large ball will allow very young players to safely experiment with spin. By brushing up along the side of the ball or down under it while the coach holds it with his index fingers letting it spin, the players will be able to experience firsthand what it means to spin an object. The size of the ball and its slow movement provide excellent feedback to the players.

Use a Large Light Ball.

Use the Palm of the Hand

Using the palm of the hand of your non-hitting hand to press the ball against the strings provides a great platform for novice players to understand spin. From this position the player can move the racquet up or down, keeping the hand still, and observe the ball's rotation.

Use the Palm of your Hand.

Bounce and Spin

A good way to introduce the slice is by having players toss the ball up, let it bounce and then try to make the ball spin by using a chopping motion with their racquet across the bottom of the ball. Once the players are able to make it rotate, they can try to keep the ball in the air without letting it bounce by constantly chopping under the ball with spin.

Use the Net Tape.

Use the Net Tape

By pressing the ball against the net tape with the racquet and then brushing up to drop it to the other side of the court, the player can feel the concept of hitting up on the ball to make the ball rotate forwards.

Use the Frame of the Racquet

One of the easiest ways to introduce spin is to instruct the player to hit the ball with the frame of the racquet. For topspin, ask the player to try to hit the incoming shot up to the sky with the upper part of the frame. Then instruct the player to use the same

Use the Frame as reference.

swing but to brush behind the ball as opposed to hitting with the frame. This concept of brushing up can be emphasized by having the player stand very close to the net and hand feeding balls right in front of him. The player on the other side will have to swing up on the ball to avoid hitting the net with his follow through.

One can use the same concept for serves. For a slice serve, have the player try to hit the ball to the other side of the net with the frame using a service motion, leading with the edge of the racquet. Then ask the player to use the same swing but brush the side of the ball.

OTHER SPIN DRILLS

Once the players are able to hit the ball with different spins, use the following drills to perfect their control of spin.

Slice
Instruct players to rally hitting only slice. As they improve, they can rally trying to keep the ball past the service line, then, they can alternate between shots bouncing before the service line and past the service line.

Topspin
Ask players to rally hitting only topspin. As the players become better, they can alternate hitting one flat shot, one shot with slight topspin and one shot with maximum topspin.

Practice topspin variations.

Topspin and slice
Have players rally alternating one slice and one topspin shot.

Low, High, Very High
With the same racquet head speed, the players rally trying to hit one ball low over the net, one high over the net and one very high over the net. The players will have to hit the ball with incremental amounts of topspin to keep it in the court. Make sure the swing speed remains high and constant.

Teach control with slice.

Long, Middle, Short

Players should rally crosscourt hitting a deep shot, an angle just past the service line, and an angle landing before the service line. Just as in the previous drill, the players will have to hit the shots with incremental amounts of topspin. Make sure the swing speed stays constant.

Developing a feel for different types and degrees of spin is the first step toward gaining solid control over your shots. The next step is to understand how to use this control and stroke variety to become a better player.

THE FIVE GROUNDSTROKE VARIATIONS

I was lucky enough to have had the opportunity to work with the U.S. Junior National Team very early in my coaching career. My job consisted in coaching the players at different training camps in the U.S. and traveling to tournaments with them, nationally and internationally. It was a formidable experience, which not only allowed me to work with some of the most talented junior players in the world, but also provided me with the opportunity to meet and interact with many superb coaches.

I learned a great deal from Nick Saviano, Stan Smith and Tom Gullikson, who were running the USTA Players Development Program at the time as well as from all of my colleagues working for the USTA and several other tennis federations.

1993 USTA National Team Coaches: Jay DiLouie, Tom Gullikson, Nick Saviano, Stan Smith, Edgar Giffenig, Lynne Rolley, Carol Watson.

One of the first things that I realized during those years was how evenly matched most players were and how minute the ability differences between them were. In general, everyone hit the ball well, everyone moved well, everyone competed well, but the top ranked players consistently reached the final rounds while the rest fell short. It became clear that a minuscule difference in skill could make a big difference in the outcome of a match. It also became clear that the job of a high performance coach was to identify these small weaknesses and specifically focus the training to help the players improve in these areas.

EG's COACHING WEAPONS

The key word in high performance coaching is specific.

A player may have a good forehand in general, but may have problems with low balls, or handling pace, or hitting on the run, or generating pace. The better the player, the more specific the training.

This early experience led me to change the way I viewed tennis. I went from looking at a forehand as one skill to looking at a forehand as the sum of many different skills. I did the same with all the other basic strokes: backhand, serve, forehand volley, backhand volley and overhead, and this became the foundation of my teaching methodology.

After much experimentation, I arrived at the following practical scheme when working on groundstrokes. By closely examining the game of tennis, one sees that there are five essential groundstroke variations needed to play at a high level. These variations encompass all the different types of shots that a player needs in a match, either to defend or to attack. Mastering these variations will bring a player closer to achieving the stroke flexibility needed to compete at the highest levels of the game.

THE 5 ESSENTIAL GROUNDSTROKE VARIATIONS ARE:

The Neutral Shot

The neutral shot is used to build the point – to plan an attack when a player is not in an ideal position to attack but wants to make sure that the opponent is not able to attack him either.

Shoulder level shot to attack.

The neutral shot should be played between one and three feet over the net, deep in the court and with a high degree of consistency. A good way to quantify the speed at which to hit a neutral shot is by setting a goal to hit six to eight shots in a row without missing. Why six to eight shots? Simply because most points do not last longer than that. If a player hits too hard, he will not be able to hit six to eight shots in a row, and if he is able to hit several more shots in a row it means that he is capable of controlling the ball at higher speeds and therefore should be more aggressive to increase the effectiveness of his game.

The Shoulder Level Shot

The shoulder level shot is used to attack. As its name implies, it should be hit at shoulder level. It is hit inside the court, off a short and high ball from the opponent. The shot is hit with little spin and with a lot of speed. Technically, the preparation should be at shoulder level, allowing the player to hit through the ball with little spin. The final objective of the shot is to hurt the opponent.

The Off the Bounce Shot

Off the bounce shot to defend.

The off the bounce shot, or half volley, is used in defensive situations when the opponent's ball lands very close to the player so that the player is not able to back up, and when returning a first serve. In both cases, the player needs to shorten his backswing and drive through the ball using the opponent's pace. The goal of the shot is to return to a neutral situation in the point.

Use the Dipping shot against a volleyer.

The Dipping Shot

The dipping shot is used in situations when a player wants to keep the ball low over the net and wants the ball to travel short distances. This shot is used when hitting angles, passing shots or when approaching the net off a short and low ball. Technically, the ball should be hit with a lot of topspin, using the wrist and forearm and finishing low toward the pocket of the non-hitting side of the body.

The Lifting Shot

The lifting shot is used to hit the ball high over the net with a lot of topspin. A player uses this shot when in a defensive position and out of balance, to change the pace of a rally, or to hit a topspin lob. This shot should be hit with heavy topspin, steeply accelerating the wrist and the forearm. It should clear the net by six to 15 feet depending on the situation.

EG'S COACHING WEAPONS

These five groundstroke variations are the key to playing great tennis. Every single groundstroke hit during a point fits into one of these stroke variations. Any player playing from the baseline at any given time is either hitting a neutral, dipping, lifting, shoulder level or off the bounce shot. There are no other options.

One of the questions I usually get is: What about the slice? Slice shots can be used in the same way. A slice can be used as any of the five variations: neutral during a rally, shoulder height as an approach shot, dipping when the opponent is at the net, lifting when lobbing, and off the bounce when the ball lands close to the player. However, in the modern game the slice should be used as a complement to a well-developed topspin game.

By mastering these different shot types, any player will develop the stroke flexibility needed to play better tennis. A good training program has to incorporate all these groundstroke variations since they all require a different technique. A program that does not address these different shots will not prepare a player adequately.

I have heard the following story a million times:

Two coaches are talking to each other after one of their players just finished his match. One coach is narrating the match to the other one: "I cannot believe what happened. Johnny was playing great, and at 5-4 he had a match point. He hit an unbelievable crosscourt forehand, and all the opponent could do was to return a high ball that bounced in the middle of the court. He had a 'sitter' and missed the forehand. Every time it's the same story, he hits a great shot, gets the ball he wants and misses it. I cannot understand how he can miss so many easy shots."

This is a common story, but I am willing to bet that little Johnny never practices shoulder level shots. The coach probably assumes that practicing forehands behind the baseline will prepare him for any forehand shot, especially those "easy ones."

EG's COACHING WEAPONS

The reality is that a weakness in any of these groundstroke variations leaves a player exposed. A smart opponent will find the weakness, and the player will have no way to counter. A player without a dipping shot will never be able to beat an opponent who attacks the net. A player without a lifting shot will have a hard time defending, especially on clay. A player with an ineffective shoulder level shot will never beat a player with good defensive skills, and so on.

My own experience growing up is a perfect example.

Growing up on clay in Mexico, I built my game around consistency, touch and movement. When I arrived at the University of Texas, I was playing on hard courts for the first time and had a very difficult time adjusting. Playing against net rushers on fast hard courts really forced me out of my comfort zone. One of the main problems I faced was my backhand. I was very consistent with my slice but not with my topspin shot. On clay I could run around the backhand, but on hard courts I had to face my demons. I could keep the return low but had a hard time passing, which was a big part of the game in college. Needless to say, college tennis was a very trying experience, and

All great players have mastered the five ground stroke variations.

although I really enjoyed it, I did not feel comfortable on the court for the first time in my life. My weakness was exposed and my whole game was only as good as my weakest shot.

This same concept can be applied to the net game. However, the different variations are subtler.

THE FIVE VOLLEY VARIATIONS

Applying the same reasoning to the net game, these are the different volley variations that need to be practiced to achieve stroke flexibility at net:

Low Volleys

Low volleys are hit under the net level with backspin, usually using the legs to run through the shot.

High Volleys

High volleys are hit flat or with very little slice, with a longer swing, using the whole arm from the shoulder.

Stretch Volleys

Stretch volleys are hit in a stretched out position with an open racquet face against wide passing shots.

Defensive Volleys

Defensive volleys are hit against very fast incoming balls. They need a very short backswing and a firm contact point.

Low Volley

High Volley

Topspin Volleys

Topspin volleys are an important shot in today's game, especially in the women's game. These volleys are hit at shoulder level off very high and slow balls and are basically a shoulder level shot hit in the air. As with the groundstrokes, a player at the net has to be able to handle every type of shot coming at him. Working on mastering these different volley variations is essential to becoming a proficient volleyer.

OTHER VARIATIONS

The rest of the game is no exception. Here are the other technical skill variations that should be planned into anyone's practice schedule to get ready for battle:

SERVES

Serve to all directions with different types of spin: wide, middle and T

Flat Serve

A flat serve is a powerful serve with little spin.

Slice Serve

A slice serve uses sidespin to make the ball curve from right to left (for right handed players).

Stretched Volley

Practice flat, kick and slice serves.

Kick Serve

A kick serve makes the ball rotate forwards to allow the player to hit higher over the net, thus improving his safety margin. It is most commonly used as a second serve.

RETURN

First Serve Return

The tactical goal of the first serve return is to keep the server from taking control of the point. Depth and consistency are paramount to returning a first serve. One needs a compact swing to be able to contact the ball in front of the body and use the opponent's ball speed. This shot can be hit with topspin or with slice, and both variations should be practiced. Technically, the swinging pattern for a topspin return is the same as the one used in the off the bounce shot. For a slice return, the swing resembles a volley.

Second Serve Return

The tactical goal of the second serve return is to try to gain control of the point. The returner should play aggressively, with a high degree of consistency. The technique for the second serve return is similar to that of the shoulder level shot.

Chip and Charge

Chip and charge is the practice of blocking a return of serve and charging the net. This return is normally used on second serves to put pressure on the opponent in singles or in doubles. The technique is similar to that used for a volley, and special attention should be placed on hitting the return while moving to the net. The returner should start moving forward as the opponent tosses.

OVERHEADS

Off the Bounce

The key to hitting an overhead after letting a lob bounce is to position one's body well behind the bounce of the ball and adjust to the shot by moving forward. This is opposite to the typical backward movement needed to adjust to an overhead when the ball is hit in the air.

In the Air

There are two variations to this type of overhead. When the ball is high and close to the player, the player should use small sidesteps to place himself in the ideal hitting position. On the other hand, if the lob is coming fast and deep, the player needs to learn to use crossover steps and a scissor kick to adjust to the ball.

Backhand Overhead

In general, every net player should try to run around the backhand overhead to hit a forehand overhead. Sometimes this will not be possible however, and the player will have to use his backhand. Therefore, it is important that this emergency shot is incorporated into the practice schedule.

SPECIALTY SHOTS

The specialty shots are those shots that are not very common but are important because they can be used to change the momentum of the match. They give the player a chance to come back from very difficult situations or to surprise the opponent. Here is my list of key specialty shots:

Defensive Lob

This is a very high and deep lob hit with a little slice that is used when the player is in a very difficult situation against an opponent at the net. This lob should be aimed deep into the middle of the court.

Recovery Lob

This is a lob that a player uses to counter against a lob that went over his head. In this case the player has to run toward the baseline and hit a high defensive lob with his back facing the net. Especially important to execute this shot effectively is to run to the side of the ball and aim deep to the middle of the court.

Offensive Lob

This is basically a groundstroke lifting shot.

Drop Shot

A good drop shot at the right time can change the momentum of a match. It is important to remember here that the effectiveness of the drop shot will depend on the degree of disguise and not on the player's touch or feel. In addition, a drop shot will always be more effective when executed in an offensive position.

Summary
& Conclusions

As one can see, an effective tennis practice has to be well structured. The basic strokes, forehand, backhand, volleys, overhead, serve and return, need to be further subdivided to include all the shots a player might need during a match. This is the key to developing better weapons for battle (**stroke flexibility**). This is not always easy to do if we do not plan ahead. We all have drills that we tend to use over and over, and it is very easy to neglect different areas of the game. Moreover, players have a tendency to like the drills that they can do well and hate drills that they have a hard time executing. But, to develop better players it is very important to identify those areas of difficulty and work more on them.

An easy way to be sure your players are practicing every necessary stroke variation is to schedule half the practice time to work on the baseline and the other half to work at the net. The practice time spent at the baseline should cover all types of groundstrokes, and the time at the net should cover all types of volleys and overheads. The serve and return should be integrated into every practice by getting your players into the habit of starting any drill with serve and return whenever possible as opposed to starting the rally underhanded. So, if a player is going to practice a crosscourt forehand shot, he starts the drill by serving crosscourt. The opponent should return crosscourt and after that the drill can be executed as usual. By doing this, your practices will be more effective. The players will start each point the same way they do in a match, allowing them to integrate the two most important shots in today's game into most of the drills and certainly into all practices.

What kind of drills lead to highly variable practices and therefore to the development of stroke flexibility? The next section will address this issue.

STAY THE COURSE!

Tennis is a very complex game that requires many different skills, and as a coach it is sometimes difficult to cover everything. There is so much to do and so little time, and no matter what you do, you will always neglect something. Therefore, it is very easy to jump constantly from one skill to the next trying to catch up. To make things even worse, as soon as one aspect of the game improves, often another one starts to deteriorate.

Looking back at my career, I can remember many times when I had great ideas to help my players, but shortly after I started working on them, I found myself trying another "great idea."

I remember, for example, working with a high net to increase the margin for error and depth in my players' shots, or including some fitness drills on water breaks to cover areas that we had neglected for lack of time, or playing a set every day to get match tougher, or doing movement drills before practice to improve quickness, or many other drills that I designed to attack a major problem at the time.

The ideas were always good, but I often cut the experiment short. One week of high net is probably not going to make a big difference, but six weeks would definitely promote positive change.

Be patient, prioritize and plan your workouts long-term.

Stay the course!

DRILLS TO DEVELOP STROKE FLEXIBILITY

From the last chapter you know that achieving total stroke flexibility is the key to developing better weapons for battle, and that this can only be accomplished by incorporating all different shades of strokes into our practices: the five groundstroke variations, the five volley variations, the specialty shots and, of course, the different types of serves and returns.

You also know that all these slight variations of the basic tennis strokes have to be targeted and practiced to achieve total ball control; that you have to force your players to practice as specifically as possible; and that you have to challenge them with variability.

There are four types of drills used to build a solid flexible technical base: feeding drills, wall drills, collaboration drills and competitive technical drills. All these drills allow the players plenty of repetition for all different types of shots that they will encounter in a match.

Most coaches will be familiar with many of the drills that I will present in the next few pages, but the key to making the system work is to understand how to manipulate these common drills to make them more precise and effective in the development of stroke flexibility.

FEEDING DRILLS

A coach feeds balls to the students so that they can improve their technique through repetition, simple. They are the most common drills in tennis. However, even these simple drills can be very effective in promoting stroke flexibility, when the following guidelines are followed:

» Feed every type of ball that a player will encounter during a match and work on the technical skills needed to return the feed effectively (topspin, slice, high, low, fast, slow, deep, short, etc.). Make sure the players can hit all five types of groundstrokes, all five types of volleys, and all the other types of shots mentioned earlier.

» Force the players to move as if they were in a live ball situation. The movement cycle (split step, adjustment steps and recovery steps) should be part of all drills.

» Feed randomly after a while, even when working on a specific stroke. Do not feed to the same side at the same speed for too long. As soon as the player starts to get into a groove, vary your feeds.

- » Use targets as much as possible. Area targets like three by three feet targets are better than object targets (example: a cone) since the players will experience success more often.
- » Feed as closely as possible to the type of balls that the player will experience during a match. Do not make the mistake of feeding advanced players very easy shots, unless they are making a major change in their technique or working on putting the ball away.
- » Make sure all players on the court are active during these drills. Do not have the players wait in line for too long.
- » Try to include a tactical component in every drill whenever you can. For example: Explain to the player when and where he is supposed to hit the shot that he is practicing during match play.
- » Use a combination of feeds that mirror what the player will encounter during a point such as: a high lob after a shoulder level mid-court shot or a passing shot after an approach shot.
- » Feed from different parts of the court to change the characteristics of the incoming ball. Feed from anywhere on the court. Use your racquet when feeding from far away and use your hand to toss to a player standing close to you. Tossing balls with the hand can be very effective, even with advanced players because it allows you to have total control of the ball and the frequency of the feeds. It also forces the players to generate their own speed.
- » Feeding drills can also be very effective to work on footwork and general on court movement.

Feed every type of ball.

The wall is especially effective to practice volleys.

WALL DRILLS

Practicing against the wall is an excellent way to improve technique and develop ball control. One can practice any type of shot against the wall. The key is to be specific. Do not practice backhands, but practice specific types of backhands, such as dipping shots, off the bounce shots, etc. These guidelines will make your practices more effective:

>> Set up drills to practice all types of shot variations (neutral, off the bounce, shoulder level, etc.).
>> Make sure the movement cycle is being executed correctly in every drill.
>> Use targets on the wall to increase the demands of the drills.
>> Use movement along the wall and forwards and backwards in the drills.
>> Players should never let the ball bounce twice.
>> Players should start the rally with a serve.
>> Concentrate on the correct technical execution of the stroke as well as on consistency and accuracy.

The wall is especially useful to practice all volley variations. Here are some drills that have worked very well for me. I learned them from my good friend and colleague at the German Tennis Federation, Zdenek Zofka:

Forearm volleys

The player stands sideways in a volleying position with the racquet a few inches from the wall trying to keep the ball in play with a minimal movement of the racquet.

Step Volleys

The player stands sideways in a volleying position about eight feet from the wall. The player keeps the ball in play using volleys, simulating stepping forwards each time but actually remaining in the same place. The goal is to match the racquet/ball contact point with the foot/ground contact point.

In and out

The player volleys against the wall, moving sideways, toward and away from the wall, matching the contact point on the strings with the contact of the front foot with the ground.

Across the wall

The player volleys against the wall, moving sideways along the wall, matching the contact point with the contact of the front foot with the ground.

Two Volleys/two half Volleys

The player alternates hitting two volleys and two half volleys, moving forward and back.

High Volleys

The player practices high volleys, keeping the ball in play, bouncing the ball off the ground before it hits the wall so that it pops up after hitting the wall.

COLLABORATION DRILLS AND COMPETITIVE TECHNICAL DRILLS

The collaboration drills involve working on consistency and accuracy with a partner, and the competitive technical drills involve competing against a partner using a variety of very specific and different tasks. All these drills will be more effective if both players start the rally with a serve as opposed to starting the rally with a groundstroke.

COLLABORATION DRILLS

Collaboration drills use repetition to improve the technical skills of the players. The players execute a high volume of shots, looking for consistency in the execution and in the outcome.
The collaboration drills are basically the same old drills used in many practices over the years, with a subtle but extremely important difference: they incorporate all the various types of shots that a player could need in a match.

The new and improved collaboration drills that I propose are very specific and are built around all the stroke variations that I introduced in the last section. For example, instead of practicing crosscourt forehands, the players practice one of the five forehand variations or a combination of all of them (neutral, shoulder level, off the bounce, lifting or dipping). The same concept applies to all strokes.

To increase the effectiveness of these drills, **the players should either count the number of shots hit in a row, or try to hit a specific target while competing to see who achieves the greatest number of accurate hits.**

Here are a few examples:

Off the Bounce
Two players rally crosscourt, two feet inside the court, hitting off the bounce shots and counting how many balls they can hit in a row.

Include all the strokes in your collaboration drills.

Crosscourt Neutral Shots

Two three-foot boxes are marked on the singles court at the baseline on diagonally opposing corners. Two players play crosscourt and compete against each other to see who is able to hit five balls in the opponent's box first.

Lifting Shots

Two players hit lifting shots down the line on half the singles court. The players can only use their backhands and have to count how many shots they can hit in a row without mistakes. For more advanced players, all shots have to land past the service line.

Neutral/Dipping

One player hits neutral shots past the service line, the other player hits dipping shots that land before the service line. Players count how many shots they can hit in a row without missing.

Neutral/Off the Bounce

Two players hit crosscourt on half the doubles court. One player hits neutral shots, the other off the bounce shots; only backhands are allowed. The players count how many shots they can hit in a row without a mistake.

Dipping/Off the Bounce

Two, three foot boxes are marked on the singles court on diagonally opposing corners, one at the baseline and one in the service box. One player hits dipping shots aimed at the box in the service box, and the other one hits off the bounce shots at the service line aiming at the box on the baseline. The players compete to see who is able to hit five balls into the opponent's box first.

All these drills can be played only with forehands, only with backhands or using both shots. Demanding that the players use only one type of stroke will make the drills more challenging and force the players to move better.

The same concept should be applied to all drills in order to practice all shot variations, either at the baseline or at the net.

Here are other examples with different shots:

Overhead/Lob

One player hits only lobs, the other only overheads. A slight variation would be to have one player hit only lobs and the other only backhand overheads. Players should count to see how many balls in a row they can hit without missing.

Mixed Volleys/Mixed Groundstrokes

One player stands on the service line, the other one at the baseline. The baseline player will alternate hitting one neutral shot, one dipping shot and one lifting shot. The net player returns all shots back with control, practicing low volleys, waist high volleys and high volleys or overheads. Players should count how many balls they can hit in a row without mistakes.

There are many variations in these drills since all the following variables can be manipulated:

Shot direction: crosscourt, down the line, one hits crosscourt one hits down the line, one stands in one corner and hits one shot to the forehand and one to the backhand, both players alternate one forehand and one backhand, etc.

Size of the court: full court singles or doubles, half singles court, half doubles court, the service boxes or any other specific target area on the court.

Position on the court: baseline, net or anywhere in between.

Stroke types: players hit only forehands, only backhands, either forehand or backhand, forehand volleys, overhead, etc.

Shot characteristics: slice, topspin, high, low, short, deep, etc.

As you can see, there are an infinite number of drills that can be designed, manipulating shot direction, size of the court, position on the court, stroke types and shot characteristics. You can easily adjust the difficulty of the drill by manipulating these variables. The important element to keep in mind to make the system work is to **be specific in your demands and incorporate all of the different shots that a player may encounter in a match into your drills.**

The greater the variation, the more easily a player will adapt to new situations in the future, and the better he will be able to improvise when needed. Many emergency shots, like hitting only with the wrist because the player is forced to hit the ball behind his body, cannot really be practiced. They are the result of thousands of hours on the court adjusting to different situations. And at the highest level of the game, improvisation is what ultimately wins matches.

You will find many more collaboration drill examples in the **drill library** at the end of the book.

COMPETITIVE TECHNICAL DRILLS

These drills involve two players and are used to improve their technical ability as well as their competitive skills. They are similar to the collaboration drills and sometimes identical since they are also designed to incorporate all the different shot variations that a player may encounter or need in a match. However, the objective of these drills is to compete using the technical skill being developed, as opposed to working on consistency and precision. **The goal is to beat the opponent.** Players compete by time (whoever is winning after a certain time) or compete to see who reaches a certain number of points first.

Just as in the collaboration drills, it is important that the players start the point with serve and return whenever possible as opposed to starting underhanded.

Here are a few examples:

Neutral Shots

Two players are at the baseline competing with neutral shots (past the service line) on half a singles court down the line. Only backhands are allowed. All points are started with serves. Any mistake or short ball results in a point for the opponent.

Off the Bounce

Two players compete on half the singles court, down the line, only backhands allowed. They have to stand two feet inside the court and cannot step behind the baseline, therefore being forced to hit mainly off the bounce shots.

Use the alley to work on control.

Neutral with Pressure

Two players compete on the full singles court trying to land their shots between the service line and the baseline. The players count the number of shots (that land between the baseline and the service line) during the rally. The winner of the rally gets all those points.

Lifting shots

Both players compete hitting deep, high, heavy topspin shots at each other crosscourt on half the doubles court. Only forehands are allowed.

Variation:

If the ball lands before the service line the opponent has to attack it with a shoulder level shot, and the point opens up.

Variation:

The player has to approach the net with the shoulder level shot if the lifting shot lands short. The point is played out.

Topspin/Slice

Two players compete against each other on the full singles court. They can hit forehands or backhands but have to alternate one topspin and one slice shot.

In and Out

Two players play crosscourt on half the doubles and alternate hitting neutral and off the bounce shots by moving in and out of the court after each hit. In other words, both players hit a neutral shot from behind the baseline and step into the court to hit the next shot off the bounce inside the baseline. After each shot they move up and back, in and out of the court. Only backhands are allowed.

Forehand Volley in the Alley

Two players start at the service line but in the alley. They are only allowed to hit forehand volleys and the balls are allowed to bounce, but the players are not allowed to move back past the service line. The point is played out. The alley is the court.

Mini Tennis no Bounce

Two players start at the net. They compete in half a singles court and only in the service boxes. The ball is placed on the net strap and released. One of the players lets it bounce and plays it. After that the point starts. The ball is not allowed to bounce again. Players are not allowed to hit the ball hard or down and have to try to win the point through volley placement in the service box.

Backhand Volley/Backhand Slice

One player is at the net and one player in the back. They play crosscourt on half the doubles court. Only backhand volleys and backhand slices are allowed. The net player has to hit the volley past the service line; no lobs allowed.

Lifting/Shoulder Level

Two players compete on the full court. One hits crosscourt and the other down the line. One hits high lifting shots and the other shoulder level shots.

Just like the collaboration drills, all drills can be adjusted by manipulating shot direction, size of the court, position of the players on the court, stroke being practiced and shot characteristics.

Many of these drills are similar or identical to collaboration drills. The difference is that the players are trying to win the point instead of trying to hit a target or collaborating with the partner to achieve a certain number of shots in a row.

For drills using different shot combinations like our last two examples (lifting vs. shoulder level and backhand volley vs. backhand slice), players could alternate every two points so that both get to hit the different types of shots, or they can play the whole game using the same shot and then play another game switching off. For example, if one player is hitting neutral shots and the other is hitting dipping shots, they can alternate every two points, or one player can play the whole game hitting neutral shots and then another game hitting dipping shots.

Note: Some of the drills require the player to serve down the line as opposed to the usual cross-court serve, especially when working on half a court down the line with four players on one court. This takes a bit of getting used to, but in reality if you are serving to the T, you are basically serving on a straight line.

You will find many more competitive technical drill examples in the **drill library** at the end of the book.

All these drills, the feeding drills, the wall drills, the collaboration drills and the competitive technical drills, if designed to compel the players to experience a high degree of variability, will promote stroke flexibility and help the players develop better weapons for battle.

EG's COACHING WEAPONS

Ideally 50 percent of the drills used during a practice segment devoted to technical development should be competitive technical drills, 30 percent collaboration drills and 20 percent feeding or wall drills. I strongly believe that athletes will benefit more from hitting with each other as much as possible as opposed to hitting with a coach or returning fed balls. To excel in tennis one needs to learn to compete, so the more competitive the practices, the better.

Integrate every shot variation into your drills in every aspect of the game: groundstrokes, volleys, serves, returns, overheads and specialty shots. Analyze the drills that you normally use and see if you can tweak them to make them as specific as possible, and your players will be well on their way towards achieving total ball control.

SUMMARY
& CONCLUSIONS

Use feeding drills, wall drills, collaboration drills and competitive technical drills in your practices to develop a solid technical foundation, a great variety in the game and the stroke flexibility needed to compete. In other words these types of drills will help to develop the offensive and defensive weapons needed for battle. Use these broad drill categories to develop your own drills. In addition, try to introduce the concept of stroke flexibility even with beginners. Provide plenty of opportunities for beginners to experience what it takes to vary the speed, the height and the distance of the shot. This will set the stage early in the development process and will make learning tennis more fun, exciting and effective.

A great way to increase the effectiveness of these drills is to use them in team practices and move players up and down the courts based on their results in each drill. This is commonly called **king of the court** and it works as follows:

During competitive technical drills, players will compete in each drill for a certain amount of time established by the coach, for example five minutes. After this time, whoever is up in the score will move up half a court and the loser will move down half a court. Every drill counts, and the players are putting themselves on the line throughout the whole practice. Since all drills are very different, different players do very well in some drills and struggle with others. For example, a good baseliner may move up while the practice focuses on groundstrokes, but will move down when the emphasis shifts to net play. All drills are so specific that they will always expose a weakness. A player could have a great neutral backhand, but may have problems hitting it at shoulder level.

Drilling like this is a great way to force players to confront their demons and try to do the best they can with their limitations, while helping them to establish a very solid technical base.

Solid flexible strokes are great weapons for battle, but fast flexible strokes are lethal weapons. The next section will focus on how to help players generate more racquet head speed.

DEVELOP YOUR OWN SYSTEM

One important characteristic of a good coach is a continuous drive to improve, to seek new and better ways to help his players.

Looking back to the start of my career, I hungered for knowledge and took advantage of any opportunity to learn. I read every tennis book I could find, took all the courses and attended as many coaches' conventions as I could afford. I was searching for the best way to teach, the formula for success, and I was determined to find it.

Luckily, through my travels with the different national teams, I came in contact with many great and successful coaches with whom I was able to spend many hours discussing the game. It was a great experience that forged my teaching philosophy. However, the most important lesson for me was to discover that every coach did things differently. There were certain common elements, but there were also marked differences in their approach to the game.

The one thing all those successful coaches had in common was their firm belief in their methods. They were all passionate in their approach to teaching and had confidence in their teaching system. The secret to their success was not their superior knowledge, but a consistent approach to teaching. A method or system that they trusted.

Players improve through consistency, by practicing the same skills enough times to master them. Based on this, the best advice I can give a young coach is to work on developing his teaching system as soon as possible. He can always adjust it as he develops as a coach.

A simple plan is much better than no plan. Develop your teaching philosophy and implement it with discipline.

Introduction

With the increase in the speed of the game in the last few years the training of racquet acceleration has become essential for the success of elite players, and no discussion about player development would be complete without including this important topic.

Developing flexible strokes is the cornerstone of this training system, and racquet acceleration is an integral part of the process. Although sometimes counterintuitive, swinging fast will eventually lead to better ball control since fast-rotating balls hit with topspin tend to drop faster than slow-rotating balls. If two balls travel at the same speed through the air, the one rotating faster will always land shorter, and that is the secret of the pros. Extremely fast ball rotation allows them to control the ball at great speeds.

However, this idea is not easily grasped. I have gotten my fair share of blank stares after asking players to swing faster to achieve more control on shots that they are missing. When you are missing a shot, and the coach asks you to swing faster, your first reaction is usually to laugh, followed closely by sincerely thinking about changing coaches once you find out that he is serious. Yet it is essential to understand this concept.

One of the toughest concepts to teach young players is the notion of hitting the second serve with the same racquet acceleration as their first serve. Players tend to get tentative on second serves and slow their racquet head speed, losing control and frequently missing. Players need to learn to accelerate their racquet on second serves to achieve greater ball rotation and therefore more control, and the same concept applies to all strokes hit with topspin.

The problem for a coach is that during the development phase, when a player's technique is still suboptimal, an increase in racquet head speed will easily lead to a decrease in control, negatively affecting his game. Therefore, the coach must find a way to help players develop control and racquet acceleration simultaneously.

So far, the emphasis of the book has been on control (flexible strokes), and I have not touched much on acceleration. Here is how acceleration has to be integrated into the development process.

First and foremost, it is essential that players develop technically sound strokes that allow them to generate optimal racquet head speed, and although I do not want to spend too much time describing tennis technique in this book due to the large amount of available information on this topic, a discussion of the kinetic chain and a review of the technical principles for the forehand, backhand and serve are important at this point.

The kinetic chain is a model used by sport scientists to explain how forces are transferred in sports or, in other words, how the different body segments work together to generate an efficient movement pattern. This model can be very useful when analyzing a tennis swing.

EG's COACHING WEAPONS

In general, using the kinetic chain model, the tennis swing can be described as a coiling and uncoiling of the body that leads to a summation of forces from the legs to the racquet head. Players will coil their bodies around and down and then will push up and rotate to accelerate their racquet head. For example: to hit a forehand, a player will rotate hips and upper body and will bend at the knees on the backswing. From that position he will start swinging by explosively pushing against the ground with the legs and rotating the hips, the torso, the arm and the wrist sequentially. The final speed of the racquet head will equal the summation of forces or velocities of each of these body segments. Just like on a whip, the last segment, the tip, will move the fastest.

Load

Explode

Finish

Backhand

The following aspects should be considered when teaching a backhand groundstroke:

One handed Backhand

Grip
>> Start young beginners with an Eastern backhand grip (index finger knuckle on top of the racquet) teaching them to hit with topspin. Introduce the slice later once the player can execute the basic topspin pattern.
>> At the beginning it helps to teach the stroke with a straight arm.

Footwork
>> Start the players with a neutral stance. Make sure their feet are perpendicular to the net. Players should step towards the net and not towards the sideline.
>> Teach the players to bend the knees to use the whole body as they hit.
>> The players should know how to rotate the body on wide balls to stop momentum after the hit.

Backswing
>> Teach the player to take the racquet back rotating the shoulders.
>> The player should use a looping pattern on the backswing.
>> Have the player rotate the torso as soon as he realizes the ball is coming towards the backhand.

Eastern backhand grip

Great balance!

Full shoulder rotation

Torso remains stable through contact.

>> Have the player keep the wrist up and take the racquet back with fairly straight arm.

>> Teach a two-step backswing. Turn torso early, pause and then swing.

Contact Point

>> Keep the contact point in front of the body with the arm straight.

>> Make sure the front shoulder remains still until the ball is contacted. Avoid the common mistake of rotating the torso too soon.

>> The head should be still at contact.

>> The shoulders should remain parallel to the ground throughout the stroke.

Perfect low to high swing.

Swing

>> The swing should be low to high. The player should drop the racquet head below the ball before contact. The player should be balanced throughout the stroke.

>> The swing should be fluid and in one continuous motion.

>> The arm rotates as it moves forward.

Follow through

>> In general, the follow through should be long towards the target. Wrist should finish up.

>> The non-hitting arm should move backwards in the opposite direction of the hitting arm.

The perfect finish!

>> The racquet head should point up at the end of the swing, and the arm should point in the direction of the target.
>> The arm should be fully extended at the end of the swing.

Ideal grip

Two Handed Backhand

The following aspects should be considered when teaching a two handed backhand:

Grip

>> Ideally, the player should use an Eastern grip (shaking hands) with the non-dominant hand and a Continental grip (hammer) with the dominant hand.

>> Introduce the slice soon after the player can execute the basic topspin pattern.
>> Have the player hit left-handed forehands to get the feel for the use of the non-dominant hand.

A great example of a closed stance.

Footwork

>> Make sure the players can hit with an open and with a closed stance.

>> Teach the players to bend the knees to use the whole body as they hit.

>> The players should know how to rotate the body on wide balls to stop momentum.

Backswing

Balance on contact.

>> Teach the players to take the racquet back by rotating the shoulders.

>> The players can take the racquet straight back or use a looping pattern.

>> Have the players rotate the torso early as they recognize the direction of the incoming ball.

>> Teach a two-step backswing. Turn torso early, pause and then swing.

Contact Point

>> Keep the contact point in front of the body.

>> The head should be still at contact.

>> The shoulders should remain parallel to the ground throughout the stroke.

Great rotation! Body uncoils and faces net.

Follow through

>> In general the follow through should be long towards the target and then wrap around over the right shoulder (right-handed players).

SERVE

The following aspects should be considered when teaching the serve:

Grip

Teach beginners with an Eastern grip and switch to a Continental grip once they are able to execute the basic service motion.

Footwork

>> The player should stand sideways to the net with his feet slightly past perpendicular to the net.
>> The player can either keep feet still or take a step with the back foot towards the heel of the front foot during the serve.
>> The players should land on the front foot after exploding up and forward.

Backswing

>> The backswing could be long, letting the racquet drop, or short, lifting the racquet to the throwing position. In both cases the key is to make sure the player is getting into a good position from which to explode, which means the elbow is aligned with the shoulder at a

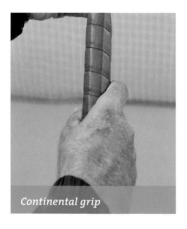
Continental grip

Loading

Pushing off and extending.

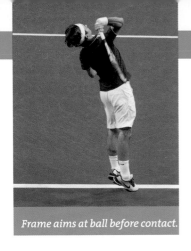
Frame aims at ball before contact.

Fully stretched on contact.

Torso stays up as long as possible.

90 degree angle to the body, the shoulders are slightly tilted, the knees bent and the upper torso coiled.

>> The tossing arm should go up slightly ahead of the hitting arm.

Swing

>> The player needs to coordinate the use of the legs with the whole swing.

>> The whole motion should be fluid.

>> The player should jump and stretch up to hit.

Contact

>> The contact point should be as high as possible with a slightly lower contact point when trying to hit a topspin serve. The ball should be contacted in front of the body, over the head slightly toward the side of the hitting arm.

>> The head and eyes should remain up through contact.

Follow through

>> The tossing arm should bend towards the stomach as the hitting arm moves up to hit the ball.

>> The racquet should follow through towards the non-hitting side of the body.

>> The torso should stay up as long as possible.

Achieving these technical elements on all strokes will allow the players to accelerate the racquet head efficiently, but that is only the beginning. Even with a solid technical base, racquet acceleration has to be emphasized in training through different drills and the ever-present mentality to continually work on generating more racquet head speed without sacrificing control.

Racquet Acceleration

It is essential that players are made aware of the importance of racquet acceleration every day during practice. Players should continually search for that thin line in which acceleration and control are in balance. In other words, players should always try to swing as fast as possible until they start losing control. This line will vary slightly every day, but in general if the player is being very consistent in practice, he should try to swing faster and see if he can maintain the same level of consistency. He should continue pushing the envelope until consistency starts to suffer. On the other hand, if a player is lacking consistency, he should try to hit with more spin first, keeping the racquet speed high, and if that fails, he should decrease the racquet acceleration until he starts gaining control.

In addition to this mindset, there are two specific types of drills that will help players increase their swing velocity.

» **Relaxation and Swing Development Exercises.** Exercises to help the players identify which muscles are really used in the swing and which need to be relaxed.

» **Pure Acceleration Exercises.** Exercises to develop the motor ability to swing fast. Their goal is pure racquet speed, without any emphasis on control.

RELAXATION AND SWING DEVELOPMENT EXERCISES

The goal of these types of exercises is to teach the players to swing effectively using as little effort as possible.

Generally, players will muscle the ball when trying to hit harder instead of letting the racquet head swing faster through the air. To swing at high speeds, the player needs to learn to engage only the muscles needed and to relax all other muscles that could slow down the swing. This can only happen if the player is totally relaxed throughout the swing. Any tension will reduce swing speed by engaging muscles unrelated to the action. It is like driving a car with a handbrake on. The car will move, but not as fast or as effortlessly as it should. The following exercises will help smooth out the players' swings.

Use easy feeds to work on relaxed acceleration.

Note: The players should be asked to breathe out while swinging during all these drills and to execute the swings with as little effort as possible.

Heavy Racquet

The player is asked to swing a racquet or similar object with more weight than his regular racquet with the minimum effort possible. For example: two racquets, a weighted racquet, a baseball bat, etc. The player should swing fast enough to hear the object cutting through the air. A heavier object will be more difficult to "muscle" so the player will have to let it swing, becoming familiar with the feeling of letting the racquet do the work.

Three Finger Swing

The player swings his racquet while holding it without using the ring finger and little finger. Then he tries to hit balls holding the racquet in this way.

EG's COACHING WEAPONS

The root of tension in any type of swing is the grip. If the grip is too tight, the player will not be able to swing efficiently.

Holding the racquet with three fingers prevents the player from overly tightening the grip and hindering movement at the wrist joint.

Three Speed Swings

The player is asked to hit a stroke at three different speeds, slow, medium and maximal, being aware of any increases in unnecessary muscular tension as the speed of the swing increases. The player should strive to achieve maximum speed with minimum effort.

All these exercises should be used often since they form the basis of a good swing development program.

PURE ACCELERATION EXERCISES

The goal of these exercises is to strengthen the muscles as well as to improve neuromuscular coordination to achieve higher racquet head speeds. Control is absolutely unimportant in these drills. As a matter of fact, these drills will probably be more effective when executed outside the court or against the fence so that the players can fully concentrate on accelerating without worrying about control.

There are two types of pure acceleration drills: contrast drills and racquet head speed drills.

Contrast Drills

These are drills in which the player´s muscles are over-stimulated and immediately under-stimulated or vice versa to force a faster than normal response. This effect is achieved by alternating the use of heavier and lighter objects. For example:

Medicine Ball Throws

Throwing a medicine ball six times, as fast as possible, followed by six maximum speed swings. This exercise can be done with groundstrokes or with serves. To improve groundstroke acceleration, use two handed throws mimicking a forehand or backhand. To improve serve speed, use overhead throws.

Alternating Weights

Alternating the use of a badminton racquet with a tennis racquet and shadow swinging each six to eight times at maximum speed, followed by six to eight groundstrokes or serves using the same maximum speed swing.

Heavy Racquet

Swinging a racquet with a racquet cover or an additional weight at maximum speed six to eight times, then shadow swinging without it and then swinging at the same speed, hitting a ball. Note: In order for these drills to be effective, all swings and throws need to be executed at **maximum speed.**

RACQUET HEAD SPEED DRILLS

These are drills in which the player learns to swing the racquet head as fast as possible. They usually emphasize forearm and wrist speed. For example:

Ball Against the Net

The player stands three feet from the net, drops a ball and tries to swing into the net as fast as possible for six to eight times. The swings should be executed with very small backswings at very high speeds.

Fast Feed Drill

The coach stands at the side of the player and tosses six to eight balls in the air one after the other in fast succession. The player is instructed to swing as fast as possible catching the ball in the air before it hits the ground. The coach's fast tempo feeds will force the player to use very fast and compact swings.

Regular Feed Drill

The coach stands on one side of the net and feeds balls. The player stands three feet inside the court and either takes the balls right off the bounce (half volley) or in the air and swings as fast as possible with great amounts of spin.

Swing like you throw – push and rotate.

SUMMARY
& CONCLUSIONS

Trying to develop racquet acceleration and control simultaneously is a challenging task for any coach. However, racket head speed is an essential component in the development of a solid technical base and should be addressed accordingly. Coaches should emphasize racquet acceleration and use relaxation and swing development exercises as well as pure acceleration exercises during practices. Remember that flexible strokes are great weapons for battle, but fast flexible strokes are lethal weapons.

So far the scope of the book has been on developing a strong technical base, or in other words, teaching the players how to hit the ball better. However, tennis is not just about hitting the ball well, but about knowing where to hit the ball for maximum results with minimum risk, and that is what the next sections in the book will address.

Keep it Simple

My coaching career has come full circle. When I first started, I had limited knowledge, so my approach to the game was very simple. I used what had worked for me as a player and applied it to my coaching. My teaching system was based on a few key concepts. Practices were very straightforward and basically consisted of drills to help my players incorporate these few concepts that I believed in into their games.

With time and experience, my knowledge base grew, and I was juggling many different ideas, trying to fit them into my coaching style. It was a period of great experimentation trying to organize all this new information: drills, facts and technical and tactical concepts floating around in my head.

With time I condensed this massive amount of data into a few simple concepts that are now the base of my coaching philosophy. Once again, my practices are very straightforward and simple, just as when I started coaching.

Effective practices do not have to be complicated. There is so much information out there that it is easy to get lost trying to cover too much. Consistency is the key to great coaching. Use variety in your drills to keep practices fresh and fun, but make sure your players are getting enough repetitions to master the skills you want to teach them.

Keep it simple!

PART III

Teaching how to use these Weapons

You will explore the second important concept of the system: how to teach your players to automatically hit the right shot at the right time, or, in other words, how to apply the stroke flexibility they are developing.

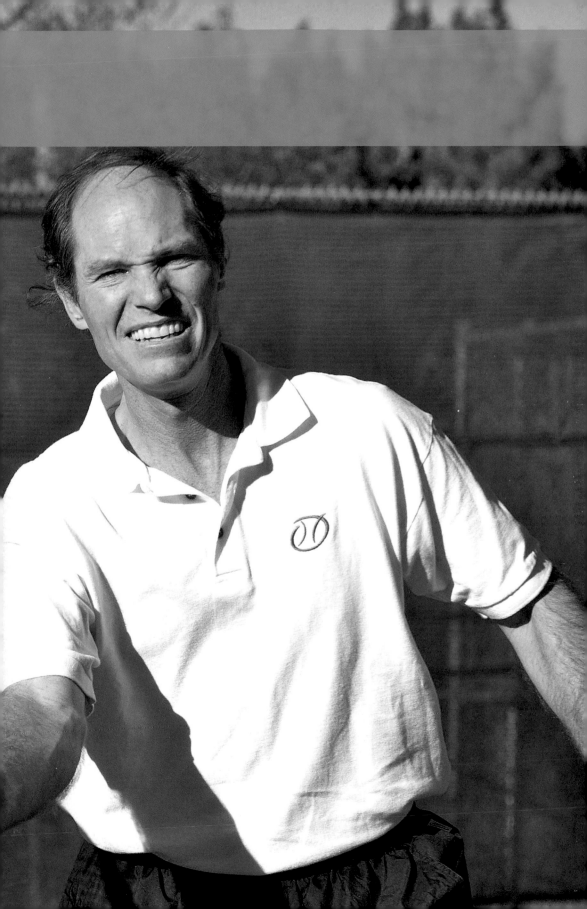

KNOW HOW TO USE YOUR STROKES MORE EFFECTIVELY

Developing solid, flexible strokes is just one part of the formula to play great tennis. Just as important is knowing how to use these strokes more effectively. A soldier can have the biggest cannon but if he does not know when to fire it, an enemy with a slingshot can defeat him.

The following anecdote exemplifies this.

As a United States National Coach one of my main responsibilities was to take the National Team to Europe during the summer to play the ITF Junior Circuit. For eight years in a row I spent my summers in Europe coaching different teams.

USTA National Team 1993.

The biggest adjustment for American players was to learn to play on clay. Most players felt very comfortable on hard courts but were not very experienced on clay. Clay courts will always expose your tactical weaknesses. The courts slow the ball enough so as to make it almost impossible to win the point through pure power. On the women's side, a great hitter may still get away with poor tactical play, but in the men's game it is much more difficult.

One of the concepts that we often used to help our players adjust was the idea of hitting yourself out of position, which basically meant that the player hit a great shot that got him into trouble.

Here are two common and recurring examples:

In the first example, two right-handed players were playing against each other. One ran around the backhand on an ad court return of serve and hit down the line to his opponent's forehand. Unless the shot was so good that the opponent could not touch it, the returning player usually lost the point, even with a great return. The reason was that running around the backhand would usually leave the player returning from the alley. From there the down the line shot would leave the whole court open for the opponent to attack crosscourt and put him on the defensive.

In the second example, a player on the run close to the alley played an aggressive down the line drive. Unless the shot was a winner most of the time the player would lose the point because hitting down the line hard would leave him out of position to defend a good crosscourt shot from the opponent.

In both cases, the players' shots were not the problem. As a matter of fact, they were very well executed shots. The problem was that they were not the ideal shots to hit in these situations. One can even argue that in both cases the better response was probably a less technically demanding shot: a neutral inside out forehand on the return and a lifting crosscourt shot on the run. These are perfect examples of having great weapons but not knowing how to use them. So, building better weapons is only part of the answer. Knowing how to use these weapons is the other part.

Playing tennis is an automatic process that requires little thinking once the point is in play. A player needs to be able to recognize a situation and come up with the ideal response automatically. To do this successfully, a player has to understand the tactical theory of the game and integrate this knowledge into his game by practicing specific drills.

The following two sections will present a detailed program on how to do this.

This section explains the Tactical Theory through the analysis of the following subjects:

>> Geometry of the court or how to cover the court more effectively.

>> Laws of the battle or the key tactical concepts of the game.

Section 7 will expand on this section and show you how to integrate this theoretical knowledge into your players' games.

GEOMETRY OF THE COURT

One of the most important tactical aspects of the game is the concept of the "Geometry of the Court," which explains how to cover the court efficiently and is an essential concept in the tactical theory of the game.

Looking at the court from the perspective of court coverage, we know that a key element of footwork is getting back toward the middle immediately after every shot. But where exactly should we recover to?

Understanding the geometry of the court will help us answer this question because the exact middle of the court is not always the ideal position to wait for the next shot.

Ideally, a player should strive to place himself in the middle of the opponent's best possible shots after each hit. To achieve this goal one has to consider both types of movements, up and back, and side to side.

Let us begin by looking at where a player has to position himself when at the baseline. Tactically, the closer a player is able to contact the ball from its bounce the better since it will save steps and will keep him closer to the center of the court (Figure one). Additionally, catching the ball early will take time away from the opponent, because the shot will return sooner. However, hitting the ball close to where it bounces is not easy and requires great footwork, perception, anticipation and coordination. It is almost impossible to do this on forcing shots from the opponent. Therefore, the ideal position at the baseline will vary slightly from player to player and from shot to shot throughout the point.

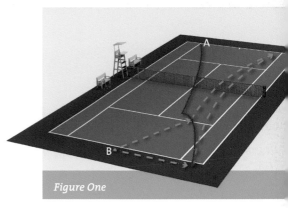

Figure One

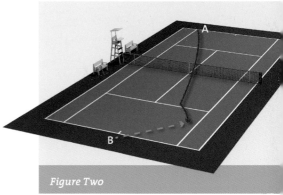

Figure Two

As a general rule, the best starting position from the baseline is anywhere from a few inches behind the baseline to three or four feet, depending on the player's ability and type of surface, but the most important thing is not where one starts, but how to continually adjust one's position depending on each shot. Ideally, the player should strive to contact the ball as it is rising, never letting it drop, in other words, moving forward, stepping into the court and catching the ball early. (Figure two).

Of course, the movement on the court is not always forwards. If the opponent's ball is very deep or far from the player, he should back up enough to be able to reach the ball or to be able to take a good swing at it.

A good exercise to practice this up and back movement is to rally trying to maintain the same distance between the bounce and the contact point on every shot. This will force the player to constantly adjust forward or backward for each shot. The ideal distance between the bounce and the contact point varies from five to seven feet depending on the individual player's ability and the speed of the incoming ball.

Figure Three

The same result can be obtained by having the players rally trying to mentally keep a constant rhythm between the bounce and the hit. The player should mentally say "bounce" as the ball bounces and "hit" as he makes contact with the ball. The player should move in such a way as to maintain the same lapsed time between both words. (For example: bounce....hit, bounce....hit, bounce....hit, as opposed to bounce..hit, bounce....hit, bounce ....hit, bounce....hit.)

Around the net, the ideal distance to the net will also vary according to the player's movement ability and the situation. Basically, the closer a player is to the net, the easier it is to cover a passing shot and the easier it is to hit a good volley as the contact point will usually be higher. On the other hand, being too close to the net leaves a player vulnerable to the lob and diminishes the amount of time he has to react.

Therefore, in determining the ideal distance to the net, a player has to consider both issues. The goal should be to place himself as close to the net as possible in a position where he can cover the lob. If he moves and jumps like a monkey, he should be right on top of the net most of the time. If, on the other hand, his movement skills are closer to those of a donkey, he should probably hang around the service line.

The ideal distance from the net will vary be-tween five and ten feet depending on the player's ability and the particular situation. The quality of the shot and the possible shot options left to the opponent should always be considered. Especially important is to back up to cover the lob after a very forcing volley that leaves the opponent in trouble. It is always easier to move forwards if the opponent decides to try a passing shot instead of a lob.

The second and most important element to consider in court positioning is the lateral com-ponent. Where should the player stand in relationship to the sidelines?

The middle of the court is not always the best place to wait for the opponent's shot. The ideal position will depend on where one's shot lands on the opponent's court and whether one is at the baseline or at the net. In both cases, the goal is to place one's self in the middle of the opponent's best possible shots. Therefore, if one observes the graphics on figures three and four, one will be able to see that the middle of the court is only the ideal waiting position when one's shot lands at the center of the opponent's court. If one's shot bounces closer to the sidelines the ideal waiting position will be either slightly to the left or slightly to the right of the center mark.

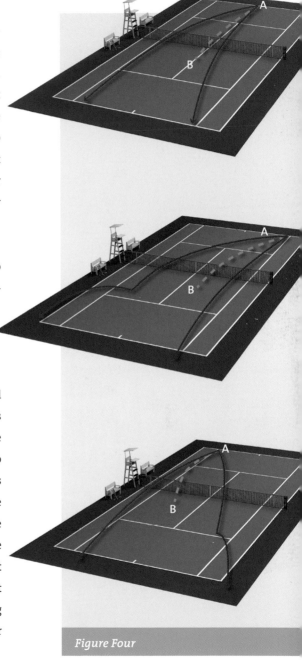

Figure Four

On the baseline, the best position to defend against a shot that landed on the left side of the opponent's court is to the right side of the center mark. (Figure three). The opposite is true for a shot that lands on the right side of the court.

At the net this concept is reversed. As you can see in Figure four, a player should position himself to the right of the centerline after a shot to the right side of the opponent's court and to the left of the centerline after a shot to the left side of the opponent's court. In other words, the body should follow the ball when attacking the net.

Understanding the geometry of the court complements the understanding of the "Movement Cycle," a commonly used term in tennis, which explains how players should move on the court. In essence it states that a player should always be on his toes and that he should split step right before the opponent hits the ball, then adjust to the incoming ball, hit and recover toward the middle of the court. The movement cycle tells us how to move, and the geometry of the court tells us where to move. (Section 8, Movement, will cover this subject in detail.)

Additionally, it is very important for the player to understand that he has limited time to get to the best possible position between each shot. He must reach the ideal court position before the opponent makes contact with the ball.

At net, follow the flight of your shot.

Therefore, the amount of time the player has to recover after each shot is the amount of time it takes for his shot to get to the opponent's racquet, not very much!

Move fast, hit, move fast, is the name of the game.

SUMMARY & CONCLUSIONS

Understanding the geometry of the court is the key to understanding the basic tactical concepts of court positioning.

Many of the "Laws of the Battle," key tactical elements of tennis presented in the next section, are derived from this concept. Here are some examples:

1. **Tactical concept: A player should always hit crosscourt unless he can hurt the opponent with the shot down the line.**
   Reason: Based on the geometry of the court, hitting crosscourt will keep the player closest to the ideal position to cover the next shot.

2. **Tactical concept: A player should approach the net with a down the line shot unless he can hurt the opponent.**
   Reason: Based on the geometry of the court, approaching down the line will keep the player closest to the ideal position to cover the opponent's next shot.

3. **Tactical concept: A player should play high crosscourt when pulled off the court.**
   Reason: Based on the geometry of the court, hitting crosscourt will keep the player closest to the ideal position that he needs to reach before the opponent's next shot. Hitting high will give him more time to reach this ideal position.

The following segment of this section will delve deeper into the tactical elements of the game and help you as a coach establish a tactical blueprint for your players.

LAWS OF THE BATTLE

This training system is unique and effective because it helps the coach accomplish three important goals:

1. **Develop stroke flexibility** in all players (complete players with better weapons) – part two of the book.

2. **Teach players to use the right shot at the right time** (complete players who know how to use their weapons) – part three of the book.

3. **Achieve consistent high-level performances** (players who can do this over and over under pressure) – part four of the book.

After reading part two (sections three, four and five), you should feel comfortable with the concept of stroke flexibility and have a fairly clear idea how to develop it. Now, the challenge is to teach your players how to use those valuable, variable shots effectively. **The "Laws of the Battle" will serve as your roadmap.**

The battle

Tennis, like everything else in life, has a set of rules that make life easier when followed but complicate matters when not. Based on my experience, I have compiled an extensive list of rules or laws that I believe to be the most important strategic concepts of the game. They summarize my understanding of the game. They describe the ideal response to any situation that a player may encounter on the court, just like a chess manual describing the best move for every position on the board. They are the theories behind the tactical aspect of the game, and the first step towards helping my players understand how to use their weapons effectively, or in other words, understand where to hit their shots in order to have the best chance of winning the point.

These rules are based on my perception of the game and may vary slightly from the tactical concepts of other coaches. However, they have served effectively as my blueprint for player development.

Having said that, the important thing is for you to understand the importance of establishing a tactical blueprint, not necessarily to agree with all the rules. To teach a player to play great tactical tennis automatically, you have to first define what great tactical tennis means, which the laws of the battle do.

Once you have your tactical blueprint, the next challenge is to continue to integrate these laws into your player's games. But first things first, let's make sure that you understand exactly what I mean by laws of the battle, by looking at a few examples. (You can find my entire strategic concept in the laws of the battle library at the end of the book.)

Use the lifting shot any time you have to back up during your stroke.

Ideally, you should always strive to move forwards to hit the ball, but sometimes the opponent's shot will force you to move backwards to hit. In this situation do not try to hit a low aggressive shot, since it is very difficult to hit that type of shot from far behind the baseline while leaning backwards. Instead, hit a high aggressive shot, deep into the opponent's court.

Always try to step into the court and catch the ball early when you have the opponent in trouble.

Catching the ball early reduces the amount of time the opponent has to move toward the middle of the court after his last shot and therefore gives him less time to cover the next shot. Good players have learned to recognize situations when their opponent is in trouble, which may lead to short balls. When this happens, they always move forward, looking to catch the ball early or even volley it to continue their attack.

As a National Coach for the German Federation, I was coaching their top junior girls who were trying to make the transition from the juniors to the pros. One of the skills that we practiced over and over was to move into the court after hitting an aggressive shot, and strive to catch the next ball early, even out of the air when possible. Invariably, when the junior girls started playing against the pros, the first thing they realized was how much better the pros defended. They did a much better job of making the opponent play additional shots even when the point was already almost lost. They were very skillful at hitting high defensive shots when totally out of position. The young girls were not used to this and lost many points after having the opponent on the ropes, by letting a high defensive shot bounce and giving the opponents enough time to regain balance.

If you run around the backhand, always start the attack with an inside out forehand. Do not go down the line with the forehand until you are in control of the point.

Running around the backhand will position you close to the sideline. Playing the shot down the line to the opponent's forehand (assuming both players are right handed) leaves you out of position to cover a crosscourt shot to the open court. When running around the forehand, start the attack inside out to the opponent's backhand and wait for a short ball to go down the line.

Use a drop shot only when you are in control of the point and inside the court. Use disguise.

Drop shots are coming back to professional tennis and are helping to make the game more exciting. They are a great way to change the rhythm of the rally and throw the opponent out of balance. They are great weapons if used sparingly and at the right time.

When you can, catch the ball early.

However, it is important to remember that a drop shot is only effective when you are able to surprise the opponent. Most effective is to hit it when inside the court in an aggressive position. The opponent will be expecting a hard deep shot and will have little time to react. If you try to hit a drop shot from behind the baseline, the shot will be harder to execute and will give the opponent more time.

Constantly look for opportunities to move into the court and catch the ball early.
Move diagonally to the ball.

Catching the ball before it drops will give the opponent less time to get into the ideal position to cover the court, which should be one of the main goals for every player. By moving diagonally to the ball instead of laterally you will constantly rush the opponent.

Vary the pace, height and spin of the rally to force a short shot from the opponent.

The more variation in your shots, the more likely your opponent will make a judgment mistake. Tennis is a game of coordination and in order to execute with consistency the player has to hit the ball at an ideal contact point. Slight variations in this contact point can lead to large variations in the trajectory of the ball. Different spins, heights and speeds likely will lead to more errors from your opponent.

These examples should have helped you to understand what I mean by laws of the battle. They are basically guidelines to solve the most common situations on the court.

The same concept should be used in doubles. Let's now look at examples of laws of the battle for doubles to help clarify the concept further.

Laws of the Battle – Doubles

Server's Partner

Most players blame the server when losing their serve, but ironically, unless the server is a master double faulter, the player at the net is probably just as guilty, if not more. As a server's partner you have a huge responsibility. Help your team by following these simple laws:

Net man is key to winning your serve.

Be active; cover a large area at the net.

Most net players believe that when their partner is serving their main responsibility is to cover the alley or to serve as cheerleaders for their partner. They crowd their alley to make sure nothing goes by and oversee their partner's performance from that vantage point. No, no, no! Be aggressive at the net; cover as much terrain as you can. Make the middle of the court yours. A good way to think about this is to try to get any ball that your partner would have to hit using his inside volley. For example: the backhand volley of a right handed player serving to the deuce court.

Your goal at the net is not to cover the alley but to draw the attention of the opponents and tempt them to hit to the alley by constantly trying to intercept their crosscourt shots.

Always consider three options when your partner serves: stay, cross, and fake. Vary your choices.

The main goal of the server's partner should be to get into the returner's head. You need to keep the adversaries guessing by constantly moving. Every time your partner serves, you need to randomly alternate between the following actions:

Stay: You will cover your side of the court.

Cross: You will try to intercept the return even if it is on the other side of the court.

Fake: You will move early towards the middle of the court to tempt the returner to hit down the line towards the alley. Then you will get back quickly to volley the down the line shot for a winner. Vary your actions and keep the returner guessing. You will win many points on return mistakes by forcing the opponents to watch you instead of the ball.

Use planned crossings.

By letting your partner know before the point starts that you are planning to cross, you can move aggressively without worrying about the alley. Since your partner knows you will cross, he will cover your side of the court.

Play close to the net if the returner is not lobbing.

The closer you are to the net, the easier it is to cover the net and the easier it is to volley. If the opponents never lob play close to the net and take advantage of all of those high volley opportunities that you will get.

Move in the direction of the serve.

When your partner is serving, your starting position should be around the middle of the service box. As your partner serves, step in the direction of his serve and split step. This movement will get you in the best position to cover the return.

By now you should have a fairly clear idea of what a tactical blueprint should look like. In section 13 you will find my complete tactical manual or laws of the battle. Use this rule compilation as guide to build your own tactical manual. Whether you use mine or your own, your next job is to devise drills that will expose your players to these situations over and over until they are able to respond to every one of the opponent's shots automatically with the shot that will give them the best chance of winning the point.

EG'S COACHING WEAPONS

Writing down your laws of the battle is a very important exercise for every coach. This will force you to analyze the game closely and identify exactly what you should transmit to your players. The exercise will provide you with a clear map, and until "tennis GPS's" are invented, your best tool to guide your players.

The next chapter will explore how to use your tactical blueprint to help your players play percentage tennis.

Cross, fake or stay!

SUMMARY
& CONCLUSIONS

Every coach needs to come up with a tactical guide for his players so that they understand what they need to do on the court in every situation they may encounter. A coach needs to break down the game into all the different situations that a player faces in a match such as serving, returning, rallying, attacking, and passing. He then needs to break down each situation into well-defined rules that the players can use every time they play. All these tactical laws need to be understood, memorized and practiced by all players until they become ingrained in their subconscious. Remember, most of the tactical responses during a match are executed automatically. A player recognizes the situation and automatically chooses the correct response.

To achieve this, the players need to constantly be exposed to all of these game situations and taught to select the correct response until it becomes automatic.

The following section will teach you how to achieve this.

Have you developed your laws of the battle?

KEEP IT FUN

Competitive tennis is a serious business that requires total commitment, and there is no way around that. It is extremely challenging and demanding, and when we are doing it for a living it is sometimes easy to forget that it is just a game, and games are fun.

Fun is an excellent motivator, and outstanding coaches find ways to make practices exciting. Of course, some practices will be more enjoyable than others, and some might not be very enjoyable, but the experience as a whole has to be positive.

An important goal for every coach should be to implement effective practices that are challenging and fun. Developing outstanding players is a long term process. Coaches need to create an environment where players eagerly show up for practice day after day.

Be creative and do not forget the FUN.

Standard Response Feeding Drill

The coach feeds drop shots and the player runs them down and hits deep down the line when forced or crosscourt when in control.

Standard Response Situation Drill

Two players are on the court playing singles. The coach feeds drop shots, and one of the players runs them down and hits deep down the line when forced, or crosscourt when in control. The point is played out.

Guided Tactical Drill

Two players play singles points. Whoever wins a point with a drop shot gets three points. The player retrieving the drop shot will win three points if he counters the drop shot down the line and one point if he wins the point by countering the drop shot crosscourt.

Doubles Laws

The same concept can be used with the doubles laws of the battle. Here are a few examples:

Law: Never let the lobs bounce unless you are facing an extremely high defensive lob.

Standard Response Feeding Drill

A player starts at the net as if his partner is serving. The coach feeds a deep lob, trying to pass him. The player reacts as quickly as possible and tries to hit an overhead. With more advanced players, you can start with the player touching the net. After a while, the coach will vary the feeds, trying to surprise the player at the net with a lob.

Standard Response Situation Drill

Four players take their positions on the court as if starting a doubles point. The coach lobs over one of the players at the net. The player reacts as quickly as possible and tries to hit an overhead. The point is played out. Similarly, players can play the point out, but with one of the players serving and the returner lobbing. If the ball bounces over the opponent's head, the point is over. With advanced players, the net man should start touching the net.

Guided Tactical Drill – Three, Two, One

Points are played out, two players at the net against two in the back. The team at the net starts the point with an underhand feed. The point is played out. Every unforced error counts one point.

Every winner counts two points. The team at the net can score three points if they are able to hit an overhead winner. The team at the baseline can win three points if the ball bounces on the other side either in front of the net players or behind them with a good lob. (Once the ball bounces, the point is over.) The game is played until a team reaches 21.

Law: Be active; cover a large area at the net.

Standard Response Feeding Drill

A player is at the net in the server's partner position. The coach feeds from the baseline as if returning a serve. The coach varies the feeds, forcing the player to cover any shot crossing the net between the doubles alley and the center of the court (lobs included).

Standard Response Situation Drill

Four players are on the court in the doubles formation. One player serves and the coach feeds a return between the center of the court and the doubles sideline. The player at the net (server's partner) tries to intercept as many feeds as possible. The point is played out.

Guided Tactical Drill

Drill 1

Four players play doubles points. Any point won by poaching counts double.

Drill 2

Four players play doubles point. The server serves and volleys. The server is not allowed to hit any volley with his inside stroke (backhand when serving to the deuce court and forehand when serving to the ad court). The server's partner has to try to intercept any returns towards the middle of the court.

EG's COACHING WEAPONS

These are only a few examples of how to design drills based on the laws of the battle that will help your players integrate these laws into their games. Once you understand the concept the number of drills that you can create is solely limited by your imagination.

When I started coaching, I used to love to go to the coaches' conferences because of all the new drills that I learned. The concept of making my own drill was a bit foreign. Drills were something you learned how to do. Creating drills seemed too complicated. However, drills are just means to practice different situations on the court. There are no good or bad drills. Drills have to be evaluated based on how useful they are in helping a player improve his game so do not be afraid to experiment. You will find many more drills that I have successfully used in the past in the drill library in Section 14. Use them and dare to create your own. You may come up with the next great drill.

SUMMARY
& CONCLUSIONS

Once a coach has established a tactical blueprint or laws of the battle, he has to use standard response and guided tactical drills to help his players integrate the tactical laws into their games, allowing them to automatically choose the best response to every one of the opponent's shots. A coach has to design drills around the laws of the battle to make sure that his players are constantly exposed to all the different situations that they will encounter during a match and know how to respond to each of them.

By doing this, the second goal of this training system is accomplished – teach your players how to use their weapons more effectively. At this point you should feel comfortable addressing the two main goals in this program: helping your players develop flexible strokes and teaching your players how and when to use them.

The following sections will focus on the third goal of the system, which is to help players optimize their game and perform consistently. This part of the book will explore three important topics: movement, game styles and pressure, which will help you further polish your players' abilities.

Technical coaching is only part of the process.

They are Never Your Players

Effective coaching requires a huge personal and emotional commitment from the coach, which leads to a pseudo-mental adoption of the players by their coaches.

Coaches like to refer to the players they are coaching as "my players," which connotes some sort of ownership. In the same way, they like to use the phrase "He stole my player," which implies that someone took something that belonged to him.

The truth is that players will seek your expertise as long as you are providing what they need at the time and will change training venues as soon as they believe someone will offer them a better training environment.

It is a competitive business, and players are always looking for an edge. Many factors influence a player's decision of where to train: number of athletes in the program, level of play, age of the participants, ratio of players to coaches, the facility, the schedule, convenience, coaching style and other personal considerations.

As a coach it is important to keep this in mind and make decisions knowing that most players are just passing through your program, especially if you do an outstanding job. If you decide to spend your own resources to help a player, keep in mind that even if you have a contract with the player, there is always a good chance the player will leave your program sooner or later.

Realistically, it is very difficult for a coach to offer the best training environment throughout a player's career. As players get older and better, their needs are totally different. They will have to travel much more, and it will be increasingly difficult to find training partners at their level of play.

It is never easy for any coach when a star pupil leaves because of the tremendous investment required to develop a top player, but it is part of the job as a high performance coach.

Players will leave. Do not take it personally. They are never your players!

PART IV

Optimizing your Players' Games to Achieve Consistent Performances

You will explore three important aspects of the game that every coach
needs to address to optimize his players' games and achieve superior,
consistent performances: movement, game styles and pressure.
These topics will round off the discussion on player development.

MOVEMENT TRAINING

Tennis is a game of movement. It is a battle for positioning in which getting to the ball in balance is essential for the successful execution of each shot. Movement is such a major component of the game that a slight change in a player's movement ability will directly affect the player's performance.

Just look at the careers of professional tennis players. As the players get older their performance inevitably declines. Rarely can players maintain their level of performance after the age of 35. This is the time when most top players start dropping in the rankings and start considering retirement. What happens? Do they suddenly forget how to hit the ball? Obviously not. The main reason for the decline in performance is a decrease in their movement ability. As they become slower they start losing the battle for positioning to younger and quicker athletes, and their shots become less effective. They start hitting more shots out of balance, losing control, power and as a consequence, tennis matches.

Movement training is a key element in player development.

Movement training for tennis is not speed training. It is much more specific.

The way you move has a major impact on your game. Tennis is a game of percentages where winning a few extra points during a match can make a difference between victory and defeat. Next time you are watching one of your players compete, keep track of all the points that he lost because he could not reach the ball, especially those instances when he was only a few inches away. In addition, make a note of all the points that he lost because at some time during the point he was forced out of balance and missed or was only able to float a "sitter" back to his opponent. You will probably be surprised to find out that a large percentage of the points that he lost were due to movement problems. Think about the impact in his game that a few extra inches of reach could make. How many more balls could he retrieve? How many mistakes could he avoid? How many more forcing shots could he hit? And more importantly how many additional matches could he win?

Movement is an essential part of the game, and any player serious about improving his game should include movement training in his training plan. However, before I go on, I would like to make one thing clear: Movement training for tennis does not equate to speed training. Speed is only one of the many components of on court movement. There are plenty of quick players who do not move very well on the court, and there are many slow athletes who move very effectively. What about the eighty-year-old player who always seems to know where the ball is going to land. And I am not talking here about "Yoda," for all of you "Star Wars" fans. Every one of us knows someone with this ability; players who never seem to be moving that fast but are always in position. Even at the professional level, you see this. Andy Murray is a good example.

1. Strive to Hit every Ball within your Strike Zone

This is the foundation of on court movement and that is why I started with this rule. Tennis is an open skill game, which simply means that each shot that you hit is different. In order to execute an effective shot a player has to analyze a variety of factors such as speed, height and spin of the incoming ball and adjust his swing accordingly. Therefore, during the course of a match the average player is executing several hundred variations of the five basic stroking patterns (forehand, backhand, forehand volley, backhand volley and overhead), and this is what makes the game so difficult. Learning to hit a backhand is one thing, but learning to hit several hundred different types of backhands is a whole different story. However, that is what tennis is all about: taking what the opponent gives you, making the necessary adjustments and coming up with the most effective response. So how does this apply to movement?

As you can see, all this variation from one stroke to the next enormously increases the degree of difficulty of the game. How much easier would it be to hit the ball if the ball came exactly to the same spot, at the same speed and with the same spin every single time. Just think who would make fewer mistakes, a player tossing the ball and hitting it, or the same player retrieving balls hit to him from the other side of the court. The answer is obvious, and this is where good movement can make a big difference. Good movers will adjust to the ball better and will be able to contact the ball at the ideal contact point more often.

The ideal place and stance to hit the ball will vary from player to player. Many factors determine this, such as stroking pattern, grip, strength, height, etc. However, once this ideal hitting position and contact point have been established, a player with good moving habits will be able to meet the ball more frequently in balance and miss less than a player with poor movement ability.

So, how does a player find the ideal contact point and stance?
The easiest way to do this is by trial and error. Take a player to the court and go through one stroke type at a time. Hit forehands for a while, then hit backhands, then move to forehand volleys and so on. As he hits each stroke, have him focus on his feet and notice which stance feels best. Once a player feels comfortable with a certain stance, have him try to hit with that stance every single time. If he continues to feel comfortable in that hitting position, he has found the ideal hitting position for that stroke. On the forehand side the ideal stance could be anywhere between an open stance (facing the net with the imaginary line between your feet parallel to the net) and a closed stance (the imaginary line between your feet perpendicular to the net). Make sure your players

Hitting in balance is half the battle.

are not stepping across their body beyond the perpendicular line between their feet and the net, since this position will prevent them from transferring their weight effectively. On the one handed backhand, the ideal foot position is somewhere around the closed stance (the imaginary line between your feet almost perpendicular to the net). On the volleys, the player should step forwards as much as possible. However, many times the player will have to step across the body to reach the ball.

Once your players find the ideal stance for each stroke, they should keep trying to reach it throughout practice and change their focus towards the contact point, going through the same process again. They should experiment with different contact points until they find one that works for them. Their ideal contact point should allow them to swing at the ball comfortably, maintaining their balance throughout the stroke. To test their ideal contact point, have them set up, swing and freeze their body after the follow through without having to move their feet to maintain balance. If they can swing freely without having to move their feet, body or head to adjust to the ball as they swing, they have found their strike zone or ideal contact point.

EG's COACHING WEAPONS

Obviously, hitting every ball in their strike zone is impossible. However, striving to do so will help the players create excellent movement habits that along with the rest of the movement laws will improve their overall game.

2. Maintain an Ideal Intensity Level

To move effectively on the court a player needs to maintain a certain energy level that will allow his body to move quickly and powerfully on command. He needs an alert mind and an ideal amount of tension in his muscles. Too much or too little muscle tension will slow him down. If you want your players to be faster on the court, they have to act the part. They have to try looking and feeling ready to run anything down every time they are on the court. I am always amazed at players who complain of being slow on the court, but at the same time look as if they were asleep when playing. If a player wants to reach more balls, he has to get ready to move. Get on his toes, bounce around and fight. Prepare himself for the best possible shot from the opponent every single time. He cannot allow himself to be surprised. That way if the opponent hits a "screamer" he will be ready, and if an easier shot comes his way, he can always adjust.

Run for every ball!

Getting on your toes and bouncing in place between hits is a good habit to help you maintain the necessary level of intensity. It is always easier to move explosively once you are already in motion. A good analogy would be that of pushing a car. When you first attempt to move the car, you encounter a lot of resistance, but as soon as the car starts to roll, the task becomes much easier. The same is true for the human body. If you are just standing on the court, you are automatically slowing down your first step to the ball. However, if you stay on your toes, your initial response will be much faster. By remaining in motion, I mean staying on your toes. You do not have to break into a frenzied Latin dance; a continuous transfer of weight from one leg to the other will suffice. Have your players experiment with different degrees of movement between hits until they find their ideal intensity level. However, once they find it, they have to make it a habit to work at that intensity level every time they are on the court.

3. Attempt to Reach Every Ball Regardless of Where it Bounces

JUST MOVE. Effective movement in tennis requires early perception and early response. That is, the sooner one is able to determine where the opponent's ball is going to land and react accordingly, the better one's chances are of reaching the ball in balance. There is no time for analysis once the opponent hits the ball. Either move or kiss the point goodbye. However, most players love to conserve energy. Why run to the ball if they are not going to get it? Undoubtedly, players like to know that they will reach the ball before they start moving, and so they develop this mental map of shots that they think they can reach and those that are probably too far away. So every time the

the ball very early, but without the depth element, reaching the ball in balance will be impossible. **Never let a lob bounce and fight hard to hit an overhead. Avoid hitting backhand overheads.**

The best way to master a backhand overhead is slow feet. Most top players will hardly ever hit that shot because they know how much more effective it is to hit a regular overhead. A backhand overhead should only be used as an emergency shot. Players should work hard to get under the ball, and they will have a much better chance of winning the point. Moreover, a player should never let a lob bounce unless it is very, very high. Letting the ball bounce will become a defensive situation and will boost the confidence of the opponent. There is nothing more reassuring than knowing that you can use the lob successfully on an opponent. Let's face it, lobbing is one of the easiest shots in tennis, and winning points consistently with a lob is every player's dream. Make the opponents work for each point. Force them to hit the tougher shot by fighting to cover every lob.

4. You Should Always Expect the Ball to Come Back

HIT AND MOVE are the key words in this section. Teach your players to look for the next shot as soon as they hit. They should never pause; there is no time to admire their work during the point. They should always try to reach the ideal court position as soon as possible after finishing their stroke and avoid analyzing their shot, JUST MOVE. Whether their shot was good or bad, they have to assume that it will come back and keep the same intensity.

After every shot, there is an ideal court position they should strive for. This position will vary according to where their shot lands, but ideally they should place themselves in the middle of their opponent's best possible shots as explained in the geometry of the court section.

Players should pay particular attention to the following situations, which depict instances where players usually let their intensity drop in the middle of the point:

1. After hitting a forcing shot that will most likely win the point.
2. After hitting a bad shot that will most likely lose the point.
3. After hitting a passing shot.

Efficient recovery is one of the most important elements of effective on court movement. In the next section I will analyze this important movement element in depth.

Always be ready!

line and should start moving towards the net as soon as the coach tosses the ball up. The net player should keep his mind alert and be ready to react to the shot. As the coach starts his swing, the athlete should split and move in the direction of the shot. If you find that the net player is not able to move toward the ball every time, he is either not timing his split correctly or is landing out of balance. Practice this periodically and ask the player to apply it in his matches. You will definitely see a difference once the player understands the concept of "Don't guess, just move."

3. First Step and Adjustment Steps

Our next stop on the road to better movement is the first step. Once a player feels comfortable with his split step, he needs to focus on improving his first step. Tennis is a game of short, powerful sprints. The distances covered by the player when running to a ball hardly ever exceeds six to twelve feet. Therefore, a player never really reaches full speed before having to slow down to hit. For this reason, a quick start is essential to improve the chance of reaching the ball in balance. Running speed, although important, is secondary to an aggressive move towards the ball.

Think of the first step as an extension of the split step. As soon as the player lands on the balls of his feet he is gone, lowering his center of gravity and pushing forcefully against the ground to explode in the direction of the incoming shot.

A common mistake of many players is timing their movement to the speed of the oncoming ball. If the ball is coming slowly they will move slowly, and if the ball is coming faster they will move faster. They will move at a speed that will allow them to intercept the ball just as they take their last step, failing to give themselves any room for error in their perception.

A player should start every movement to the ball explosively, and then adjust for differences in the speed of the incoming ball. Move fast and then slow down to hit. Players have to get into a habit of moving quickly to the perceived destination of the incoming shot and use the extra time to make minor adjustments that will allow them to be perfectly balanced during their stroke.

To summarize, taking an explosive first step to the ball will increase your players' chances of reaching their ideal hitting position. It is very difficult to accurately perceive the exact speed of the incoming ball. A hard hit ball will always be unreachable when a player uses a slow first step. Having an explosive first step, on the other hand, will ensure proper position regardless of the speed of the incoming ball.

Great movers reach the ball in balance.

A good mover will always start fast and then adjust if necessary.

Here are a few drills that will improve the first step. Please go through these drills in the order that they are presented since they build on each other.

For the first drill, the coach stands at the service line with a basket of balls, and the player will position himself a foot behind the baseline in the middle of the court without a racket. The coach will toss a ball up and feed it in any direction. The player should split step as the coach starts to swing and try to position his body right behind the incoming ball so that he ends up catching it with both hands right in front of him. The sooner the player is able to place his body in the desired position the better. The object of this drill is to teach the player to move his body quickly into a position where he is waiting for the ball. Start with some easy feeds and make them tougher as the player gets more comfortable with the drill.

The starting position for the second drill is the same as the starting position for the first drill. The only difference is that this time the player is on the baseline with a racket. Start the drill sinking down after rotating and planting the outside foot will allow him to remain balanced and stop his momentum more effectively. Once the player stops his body, the next step is to move back into the court as quickly as possible, and here is how this should be done.

Normally, if the player hits his shot close to the middle of the court, he should use side steps to recover towards the middle of the court. He should always face the opponent unless he finds himself in a position where he has to guess the direction of the next shot (for example if the opponent is getting ready to hit a short, high ball). In this case, the player may have to guess and start running as soon as possible in the direction where he thinks the ball will be hit.

On the other hand, any time a player is pulled wide, off the court and close to the sideline, he should recover with one or two explosive crossover steps followed by side steps. (A crossover step is simply bringing your outside leg over your inside leg as you move laterally.) Using a good crossover step as your first step on extremely wide balls is more efficient. A crossover step will allow you to move faster back towards the middle of the court.

Remember, a player should try to reach an ideal court position before the opponent starts his swing. Once the opponent starts swinging, the player needs to cease any lateral movement and split step in order to be balanced and ready for the next shot. So, as you can see, somewhere between the end of the recovery phase and the start of your opponent's swing a new movement cycle starts, and the whole process repeats itself.

Here are some drills to work on the recovery:
The first exercise is for the player to practice stopping his body momentum as quickly as possible on wide balls. Practice without a ball first. The player should start in the middle of the court and run to one sideline pretending to hit a shot. Make sure he finishes his hit facing the net with both feet parallel to the baseline. If he hits with an open stance this will happen automatically, but with a closed stance, make sure that he rotates and plants the outside foot to stop his body's momentum. Repeat the shadowing to the other side. Be careful on the backhand side, especially if he hits a one handed backhand. Make sure he rotates after the hit and not in the middle of the stroke. Rotating too early will negatively affect his stroke. Once he feels comfortable doing this, add some side steps to recover back to the middle. Stopping his body and recovering should flow together into one motion.

The ability to change directions smoothly and efficiently is the hallmark of great players.

definition for anticipation is: to have information about the possible trajectory of the ball before the opponent actually hits the ball.

There are three ways in which a player can anticipate a shot: cues from the opponent's swing pattern, cues from specific game situations and the opponent's tendencies.

Cues from the Opponent's Swing Pattern

Countless studies have shown that there is a marked difference in the cues that advanced players and beginers heed to while playing. Using vision-tracking devices, it has been proven that beginners focus mainly on the ball or on the opponent's racquet at contact, while advanced playes focus on other parts of the body, extracting useful information.

Some of the main cues in the opponent's swing pattern that will ultimately determine the characteristics of the incoming ball are: his stance (open, square or closed), the racquet head (open or closed), the timing of the contact point (late, on time or early), the swing pattern (low to high, high to low, short, long, fast, slow, etc.)

Skilled players interpret all of these elements to determine effectively the possible traits of the opponent's shot. A player with a closed stance, an opened racquet head and a short high to low swing will probably not be able to hit an aggressive crosscourt passing shot.

Cues from Specific Game Situations

Each situation will facilitate certain shots while hindering others. There are only a few viable shot choices for every situation on the court. Of course, this is assuming that you are playing to win as opposed to playing for the glory of making an impossible shot regardless of the outcome.

For example: A high, short ball will allow you to hit aggressively from the middle of the court to try to finish the point, while a very low, short ball will force you to hit a more conservative approach shot. The same holds true for every possible on court scenario. Therefore, an experienced player will recognize different situations and will be able to anticipate possible outcomes.

Opponent's Tendencies

Every player has favorite shots, and it is your job as a player to identify your opponent's favorite shots during the match and cover them accordingly. For example, a player may have to shift his

Learn to identify your opponent's options in each situation.

starting position on the return against a player who loves to serve out wide, or he may have to remind himself to be ready to cover the great crosscourt passing shot from his opponent.

Every player shows tendencies, and better players use this knowledge to their advantage. Great players use all these elements to help them anticipate the opponent's shots. It is an unconscious process based on thousands of hours on the court. Like great detectives, they are able to look at the picture of every on court situation and extract the relevant clues that will help them anticipate their opponent's shot.

Learning to anticipate takes a long time, and it is basically a by-product of experience. However, good coaching can accelerate the process.

Here are some things the coach can do:

Point out the Cues that the Players Should Look for when Playing

As a coach, it is sometimes hard to understand how our players can fail to recognize an obvious shot from the opponent. However, when this happens it is important to point out to your players the cues that helped you to predict the opponent's shot, and to remember that the only reason you were able to recognize these "obvious" cues is because you have spent much more time on the court and have been exposed to the same situations over and over.

Describe Specific Situational Cues as Part of your Laws of the Battle

There are certain situations during a match that frequently lead to similar responses by the opponent, because these responses are either the best possible response, the easiest response or the only possible response left to the player. These situations have to be integrated into the laws of the battle and practiced accordingly. Here are a few examples from the laws of the battle library in which the law is used to alert the player about probable shots from the opponent.

1. After your first serve, look to move into the court to attack a short return.

2. Vary your position to adjust to the server. Cover his favorite shot.

3. Always try to step into the court and catch the ball early when you have the opponent in trouble.

4. When you attack the net with an inside out forehand cover the down the line passing shot.

5. After a passing shot, move diagonally into the court looking to catch the volley early.

In all these laws, a player is instructed to look out for a particular shot – in other words, to "anticipate" the most likely response from the opponent.

Practice Situation and Guided Tactical Drills Frequently

Situation and guided tactical drills are exercises designed to extensively expose players to all the different situations they will encounter during a match until they are able to recognize each situation and automatically execute the shot that will give them the best chance of winning the point. Practicing these types of drills often will not only improve the players' shot selection but will also have a very positive effect on the players' anticipation ability. The constant repetition of the same situation will teach players which shot combinations they are most likely to encounter in different stages of a point.

Encourage your Players to Play Matches as Often as Possible

Nothing is better than match play to improve anticipation skills. A match is nothing more than a series of situations that appear over and over. In its basic form each point is a combination of serving, returning, rallying, atttacking or defending. The more the players play, the quicker they will learn about likely answers to each of their shots.

Taking these steps will help you improve your players' anticipation abilities, but it is a long process and there are few shortcuts.

Movement training has to be an integral part of high performance training because of its tremendous impact in the game. Beside the athletic factors that can be improved off-court such as: strength, power, endurance, speed, agility and flexibility, and which are not part of the scope of this book, there are important tennis specific factors that every aspiring competitive player should constantly strive to polish such as: tennis specific movement (the movement cycle), the mental approach to on court movement and anticipation.

Moderate improvements in these areas can lead to a substantial boost in performance.

Movement training is one of the three important elements that will help optimize your players' performance to achieve consistency. The other two are choosing the ideal game style for your players and teaching them how to deal with competitive pressure, which are the topics of the next two chapters.

Incorporate tennis specific movement training.

Do not Forget the "Bad Ones"

High performance coaches seem to have selective memories when recalling with whom they have worked. Over and over you hear coaches mention all the great players whom they trained, excuse me, not only trained but "made," as if players were gingerbread men.

Sometimes you hear the name of a player associated with so many coaches that you have to wonder how a player could have been in so many different places at the same time.

The reality is that "making a player" is a term that is way too loosely used in the high performance arena. Coaches tend to brag about making a player if they coached him for some time, hit with him, know him, have seen him train and, in some cases, even living close appears to license them to use the term.

On the other hand, one hardly ever hears coaches talk about all the less successful players whom they actually trained, especially the ones at the bottom of the pack.

As a high performance coach, the norm is for most of your players to underperform, at least based on their expectations. Anyone in a competitive program dreams, at some point or another, to be a highly ranked professional but very few achieve this goal. After all, there are only 100 players in the world ranked in the top 100. Therefore, the success rate of a high performance coach is extremely low, which may explain why so many coaches try to ride the wave of success when they have the chance.

However, it is important to remember that behind every exceptional player whom you trained, there are many others whom you were not able to help as much as you would have liked. These athletes are the ones that keep you grounded and serve you as a reminder to keep striving to improve.

An objective evaluation should include all the players that you coach not only the extraordinary ones.

Enjoy your sucess but do not forget the "bad ones."

Finally, a third strategy that may work but could be risky is to try to be extra aggressive – going for winners as soon as possible, not allowing the counterpuncher to find his rhythm.

AGGRESSIVE BASELINER

The aggressive baseliner is a player who is always looking to attack. He is normally very powerful and has one or two weapons to hurt his opponent. A great aggressive baseliner is:

» **Mentally:** intense, has good body language, is aggressive and very decisive.
» **Physically:** big, strong, and explosive.
» **Patterns and playing skills mastered:**
  » He has a good first serve to hurt any opponent and take control of the point, attacking a short return.
  » He is able to attack second serves.
  » He plays inside the court as much as possible, catching the ball early.
  » He has mastered the concept of rallying crosscourt and attacking down the line.
  » He uses the inside out forehand effectively, opening the court inside out and finishing down the line.
  » He has mastered the shoulder level shot to attack short high balls.

Playing an Aggressive Baseliner

This player is not very patient and will look for ways to finish the point fast. You need to be patient and make him play. The longer the point the better your chances are. It is very important to make all the returns and try to get all the balls back. Do not let him hit winners on you. Try to at least touch the balls. Make him go for a bit extra and force mistakes.

This player will most likely try to use his forehand as much as possible and will consistently run around his backhand. Play down the line from the backhand corner to his forehand, when he attacks with an inside out forehand. This forces the player to move to the forehand side of the court and away from his favorite spot on the court, the backhand side. It will also make it easier to hit to his backhand on the next shot.

An aggressive baseliner does not miss an opportunity to attack.

Net rusher

The net rusher is a player who tries to get to the net as often as possible. We used to call this type of player serve and volleyer when players used to attack the net after every serve. This is no longer the case. However, net rushers like to force the opponent and finish the point at the net whenever they have a chance. Here are his characteristics:

》 **Mentally:** decisive, confident, courageous, and persistent.
》 **Physically:** agile, tall, good reflexes, quick, good anticipation, good hands.
》 **Patterns and playing skills mastered:**
  》 He has a solid first serve. Makes a high percentage of first serves.
  》 He has an excellent second serve with good depth.
  》 He has good control, placement and spin variation in the serve.
  》 He has mastered all types of volleys and half volleys.
  》 He is very effective covering the lob.
  》 He uses the following patterns very well: serving wide and volleying to the open court or serving to the T and volleying behind the player.
  》 He is able to angle off volleys.
  》 His basic pattern off the baseline is to rally crosscourt consistently and look for a short ball to come in down the line or middle or to the opponent's weakness.
  》 He has a good slice.
  》 He understands and has mastered the chip and charge.

Playing a Net Rusher

A net rusher feels a lot more comfortable at the net than on the baseline and that is where you need to try to keep him. Try to make a large percentage of first serves and hit second serves into his body to prevent him from chipping and charging. It is very important to always make him volley with your consistent returns and passing shots.

On second serves it might pay to take some risks and go for power returns to keep the net rusher on the defensive and thinking twice about coming in on second serves. Make the net rusher volley as much as possible, using two shots to pass. Do not go for a winner on the first passing shot.

Mixing in lobs is essential to keep him from standing very close to the net, which would make it harder to pass him. Finally, it may help to attack the net more often to prevent him from doing it first.

The net rusher must master the slice.

Complete Player

The complete player is the most flexible player. He feels just as comfortable at the baseline as at the net and is able to adjust his game according to the opponent's characteristics. Here is his profile:

» **Mentally:** intelligent, analytical, flexible, and able to change focus and emotional state according to needs.

» **Physically:** very athletic, above average in all areas.

» **Patterns and playing skills mastered:**

He has mastered all defensive and offensive patterns and has a very good understanding of the basic concepts of the game, such as:

  » Rallying mainly crosscourt and attacking down the line.
  » Stepping into the court whenever possible.
  » Using short balls to change direction or use angles.
  » Mixing serving and volleying with staying back.
  » Chipping and charging occasionally to pressure the opponent.
  » In addition, this player has a very complete game; masters all different types of shots and spins and knows when to use them. He is effective playing offensively as well as defensively.

Playing a Complete Player

This player is able to play at the net or at the baseline and usually will present no weaknesses but generally has no outstanding strengths. This type of player will try to impose his game on his opponents, exploiting their weaknesses. Against this type of player the most important tactic is to find a way to impose your own game to be able to use your strengths against his weaknesses.

In general, regardless of the opponent, the first priority for any player is to impose his game style on the opponent. The next step is to make slight adjustments to exploit the opponent's weaknesses or to adjust to a different surface. It is impossible for a player to drastically change his own game based on his opponent's game or on the court surface. A net rusher might stay back a few more points in a set on clay or against a very good passer but cannot successfully play like an aggressive baseliner. Likewise, a counterpuncher will not be very successful trying to become a net rusher when playing on grass. He may try to get to the net a bit more often than 'once a match to shake hands,' but changing his style completely will only lead to a terrible performance.

Therefore, it is extremely important for any coach to guide his players and help them determine what game style best fits their individual characteristics. Work on developing these technical, tactical, physical and mental skills needed to succeed with that particular style. A coach should pay particular attention to his players' physical and mental characteristics since they are mostly innate and not very malleable.

Any player may be able to slightly change some of his physical characteristics through training such as strength, speed, flexibility, agility and coordination, but major changes will be almost impossible to achieve. In other words, a slow player can become faster with training, but he will never be as fast as a player who was born with fast twitch fibers. Moreover, a short player will never become tall, even with the best training in the world. Along the same lines, personality traits, although a little more flexible, are also difficult to mold. A timid player could become bolder through practice but the original tendency towards caution will always be present. Therefore, in choosing an appropriate game style the first question a coach needs to answer is: Does my player have any physical characteristics that limit his ability to play effectively with a given game style? For example: If the player were slow, being a good counterpuncher would be out of the question. It may be easier to work on developing weapons to become an aggressive baseliner. If the player is very small, it may be difficult to play effectively as a net rusher so it may be easier to develop as a counterpuncher.

After analyzing the physical aspects, the next step is to look at the mental aspect (personality) since it is the next hardest characteristic to change. If a player is very decisive and impatient, it will be difficult for him to play long points so he needs to play a game style that allows him to be aggressive and take chances.

Finally, the coach needs to look at the player's technical and tactical skills and determine what he needs to develop to play the chosen game style effectively. This set of skills is totally flexible and within the reach of every player so it should be the last characteristic to look at when choosing a game style. Nevertheless, understanding and mastering the technical and tactical tools needed to play the chosen game style is vital.

Physical and mental characteristics dictate the chosen game style.

To summarize and from a practical standpoint, the best way to proceed might be to start by evaluating a player as follows:

Physical Characteristics:

Height: tall, medium or small

Strength: strong, medium or weak

Speed and Agility: fast, medium or slow

Endurance: high, medium or weak

Mental Characteristics:

Confidence: high, medium or low

Patience: high, medium or low

Aggressiveness: high, medium or low

Analytical Skills: high, medium or low

Persistency: high, medium or low

Mental Flexibility: high, medium or low

Technical/Tactical Characteristics:

Weapons: What are his weapons?

Weaknesses: What are his weaknesses?

Favorite Patterns: What are they?

In what situations is he most comfortable: when the opponent attacks, when the opponent plays long steady rallies, when he is controlling or defending, when he is serving or returning, etc.?

In what situations is he least comfortable: when the opponent attacks, when the opponent plays long steady rallies, when he is controlling or defending, when he is serving or returning, etc.?

After this evaluation and based on the above description of the essential characteristics needed to succeed with a given game style, the coach and the player should proceed to choose the game style most suited for the player and work on developing those areas in which he shows weaknesses. Still, this is only the beginning of the process. Once you designate a suitable game style for all of your players, you have to be even more specific and teach them how to optimize their strengths within the chosen game style. Each athlete's playing system has to be individualized. Every player is different. You may pick the aggressive baseliner game style for several of your players, but each one will approach it slightly differently. While one of the players will be very successful building his game around his awesome forehand, another may be better off setting up his incredible down the line backhand. The third one might lose out by failing to use his serve as the pillar for his game.

It is your job as a coach to identify these differences and help all your players polish their game style even further to accentuate their strengths and protect their weaknesses.

Along the same lines, in addition to the basic patterns that need to be mastered to effectively play each of the four basic game styles each player has to develop individual patterns around his own strengths. For example, a player with a big forehand obviously needs to work on running around the backhand, hitting forehands inside out and inside in, feeling comfortable with shoulder level shots and being aggressive. At the same time, he also needs to work on other areas of his game that will help him use this weapon more effectively, like a strong first serve to force short returns that he can attack, a running crosscourt forehand that will keep him in control of the point when the opponent forces him out of his favorite spot on the court, the backhand corner, and a well disguised drop shot to use as a change-up.

As you can see, an all around flexible game and a solid tactical understanding is not enough to become an elite player.

EG's COACHING WEAPONS

The final challenge is to optimize each player's game by putting the puzzle together and devising specific and individualized patterns of play for each athlete.

This is where coaching stops being a science and becomes an "art."

SUMMARY
& CONCLUSIONS

Great players have been able to individualize their games to emphasize their strengths and shield their weaknesses. Understanding the different game styles is an essential part of the process. Once the ideal game style is determined, the goal is to develop as many of the characteristics needed to be effective. Use the chosen style and individualize it to optimize each player's game.

With some players it may be very easy to do because the physical and mental characteristics may naturally be a good match for a given game style. With other players it may not be that straightforward. If you have a small quick player who is very successful as a junior serving and volleying, you may have some difficult decisions ahead of you, since that game style may only work while he is young.

Up to this point I have presented a comprehensive system to develop solid flexible strokes, integrate the tactical laws of the battle into your players' games, help them to move better and understand and pick the adequate game style for them. However, all of this is useless if a player cannot perform under pressure.

The real test of any competitive player is to be able to play his best game when it counts. There is not much money or glory in being the best practice player in the world. In the next section I will explore some ideas on how to help players perform better under pressure.

Parents are Part of the Package

Dealing with a pushy, demanding or overbearing parent is not much fun, but it is an integral part of a coach's job.

The nature of the game attracts this kind of parent. Few sports are more demanding than tennis. It requires an enormous time, financial and emotional commitment, not only from the player, but also from the whole family.

You have to have an overly driven, type A personality to take your kids to practice every day, spend the weekends and vacations at tournaments and pay a great deal of money for this abuse. Some parents even change jobs or their residences for their kid's tennis.

It is a big price to pay so it is understandable if parents get frustrated when their children are not performing up to their expectations, and since most parents have never really played tennis at a competitive level, their expectations tend to be slightly askew.

In addition, changing children is normally out of the question so the only variable they can manipulate is the coach, and if the coach is not able to make their kids play well, then it is time to find someone who can.

Do not get me wrong, most of the parents I have met throughout my career have been wonderful, but I have also encountered my fair number of challenges.

The only thing that you can do with difficult parents is to try to educate them and explain exactly what your coaching philosophy is. Many times, once they understand the development process better, they will be easier to deal with, and may even become your biggest advocates. Other times, nothing will work and the best thing to do is to go separate ways.

For better or for worse, parents are part of the equation, a very important component in a player's career. Embrace them as part of the team. After all, you are both working towards the same goal, to help the player reach his potential.

The most important goal for every player should be to eliminate any mistakes due to lack of focus on the ball or physical or mental stress. This goal should be ever present in all practices or match-situations and coaches should find ways to keep these concepts in the forefront of their programs.

Here are a few ideas on how to achieve this.

Focus

The success or failure of any stroke in tennis depends on the contact point. The big challenge for any player is to make contact with the ball in the middle of the racquet head, at precisely the right time. The only way to accomplish this regularly is with total concentration on the ball, especially as it moves closer and closer to the ideal contact point.

Most players do a relatively good job tracking the ball from the opponent's side of the court to the bounce, but have a hard time maintaining focus as the ball approaches contact, resulting in unforced errors or loss of control. The problem is compounded in the following situations:
>> Pressure situations, such as hitting a passing shot, returning a hard serve or hitting on the full run
>> Situations where the player has extra time, such as facing a high slow volley, a high slow shot in the middle of the court or a "dinky" serve.
>> Situations of transition, such as approaching the net.
>> Serve. Coaches need to remind their players that a total commitment to the ball is not only appropriate for groundstrokes but also especially important on the serve, where perfect timing and coordination of the different body segments, the racquet and the ball are essential.

In all of these instances players tend to look up too early and fail to track the ball to the contact point. These types of mistakes need to be eliminated through improvements in concentration and tracking skills.

Here are a few drills that will help.

Focus on contact even when serving.

To be a great competitor a player has to have a clear understanding of what he can do on the court and what he struggles with. Going into a match knowing exactly what your job is gives you a great advantage. If you know what kind of shot you will hit in most situations during point play, and you understand at what speed you are able to control your shots, it is easy to stay on track and make the necessary minor adjustments to play to the best of your ability. In this situation if you are missing shots that you normally make, you have to focus your attention on the mental aspect of your game: your feelings, your focus, your tension level, your thoughts, etc. The answers will be there.

On the other hand, if you do not understand your game perfectly, it is hard to search for an answer since you cannot really know what you should be doing in the first place. Are you missing shots that you normally execute successfully? Are you trying to hit at a speed that you cannot really control? Are you hitting with the right amount of spin? Are you hitting the right shot for that specific situation? Because there are too many possibilities when you do not have a clear grasp of your game, the tendency will be to second-guess yourself throughout the match and lose confidence. I remember having a coach at some point in my career who constantly gave me mixed signals. He would tell me, "Go to the net," but if I lost a couple of points, he would say, "Stay back," or "Be aggressive," followed closely by, "Be consistent," if I did not win the next few points. Needless to say it was not easy to play with conflicting ideas.

As you know, the mental aspect of the game is extremely important in competitive tennis, and sport psychologists have developed a great number of different techniques to help players, but unless the player understands his game, all these techniques will be useless.

Here are some of the drills to help your players know and understand their games better:

Slow, Faster, Fastest (Crosscourt, Down the line, Z drill)
The player hits shots in a pattern, gradually accelerating until he makes a mistake. For example: Players A and B play neutral crosscourt shots and play faster after every five shots, five at their normal rally speed, five faster and five as fast as possible.

Series of Shots at Different Speeds
This drill is similar to the previous one. The players should rally and hit eight balls in a row without mistakes. Mistakes should be penalized with jumps or any other activity. Once the players are able to consistently hit three to five series of eight balls in a row, they should increase their swing speed and repeat the drill.

Series of Shots with Different Patterns

The players try to execute series of three or four shots following a certain pattern without making any mistakes. Only the shot combinations without errors count. To make the drills more demanding, the players could be asked to complete several combinations in a row. If one of them makes a mistake they have to start over again. For example: Two players need to complete five series of six neutral shots each. If one of the players makes a mistake in the fifth shot of the fifth series, they have to start all over again.

In these types of drills the pressure is incremental, increasing, as the players get closer to finishing the targeted number of series. In addition each mistake could be penalized by some kind of short, annoying physical activity (five kangaroo jumps).
Here are a few examples of shot combinations:

Approach/Pass/Volley

One player hits a short ball, the opponent approaches the net with a down the line shot, the first player executes a crosscourt passing shot, and the net player volleys to the open court.

Inside out Forehand

One player plays two inside out forehands and one inside in. The opponent hits neutral shots back to the backhand side of the court.

Serve/Return/Attack

One player serves, and the opponent blocks the return short. The server approaches the net with a shot to the open court.

Serve/Return/Rally

One player serves to the backhand, and the opponent hits the return back past the service line. The server hits a neutral shot crosscourt, and the opponent hits a neutral shot back.

Note: Once the players complete the pattern successfully, they should repeat the drill trying to hit more forcing shots. They need to continue this process until they start losing control. These are great drills to help players understand their games better.

As you can see, there are an infinite number of drills that you can develop. Be creative and come up with drills based on your players' needs.

STRESS DRILLS

Stress drills are exercises designed to teach the players how to compete. All these drills involve two players competing against each other. To reach our objective it is important to build negative consequences for the loser into the exercise (for example: some type of physical activity, picking up the balls, buying a sport drink, etc.).

Sets Switching Racquets

Two players play a set. The coach can call any time for them to switch racquets with each other. This will force the players to learn to adjust to unexpected situations during competition.

One Serve

Players play a set with just one serve.

This drill will not only help develop a better second serve but will also teach them how to handle the pressure of facing a second serve on key points.

Variation:

Two players play a set with one serve. The player who misses the serve or the return loses two points.

Variation:

The player who misses the serve or the return loses the game.

Use consequences to increase pressure.

Three Points in a Row

You play a set, but can only win a game by winning three points in a row. This will force the players to concentrate in every point and will expose them to many key points every time one of the players wins two points in a row.

All of these drills force the players to handle added pressure in practice, simulating actual match play.

Consult the drill library for additional stress drills.

CONSEQUENCES

A discussion on how to increase pressure in practice would not be complete without mentioning the use of "consequences." I have used this tool in several of the drills throughout the book.

Using additional consequences attached to certain shots or situations is an excellent way to increase the pressure in drills or games. Here are two common types of consequences that you can use:

Add to the Value of Missing a Shot

For example: If the player misses a given shot that you are working on, he loses more than one point or even the whole game.

Have the Player do Some Physical Work after a Mistake or Lost Game

For example: If a player double faults, he has to do ten kangaroo jumps.

Choose consequences that are easy and fast to implement immediately after the action you want to target. When using physical work keep the repetitions low. It is not conditioning. Doing five pushups is meant to be mostly annoying to add pressure and is not meant to get the players in shape.

SUMMARY
& CONCLUSIONS

Learning to deal with pressure is an essential skill that has to be developed to play competitive tennis. The pressure will always be there but teaching your players how to handle it will definitely give them an edge. Use the examples above to increase the pressure in practice, and once you understand the concepts, come up with your own drills. However, remember that actual tournament pressure can only be generated through tournament play. Make sure to include a generous amount of matches in your practices and provide an extensive tournament schedule for your players. Depending on the player's age, players should play 40 to 80 competitive matches per year.

GENERAL SUMMARY

Up to this point I have presented you with a complete and structured player development program that will give you and your players a competitive edge. The core philosophy of the program can be summarized as follows:

1. Develop better weapons than the opponent (stroke flexibility) through the use of a high degree of variability in your practice and continuous emphasis on racquet acceleration.
2. Teach the players how to use these weapons better than the opponent by establishing the laws of the battle and using drills to incorporate these rules into their games.
3. Teach your players how to move more efficiently on the court.
4. Help players pick a game style suited to their physical, mental and technical abilities.
5. Teach the players to perform with consistency by using pressure drills, match play and competition.

Once again I would like to emphasize that you have to try to pursue each of these objectives at the same time. They are not sequential in nature and therefore your practices should provide a good balance between developing stroke flexibility, incorporating all tactical elements, pressure drills and match play, while at the same time offering your players a comprehensive tournament schedule.

The next two sections will address how to put everything together and make the system work better.

Keep working on your Game

I always find it strange when high performance coaches stop working on their game. It just does not make sense unless they are physically unable to do it. If you are trying to teach a skill, you should be able to perform it to the best of your ability and continually strive to get better. Coaches who neglect this area are making a big mistake.

Continually striving to improve as a player will make you a much better coach. You are a role model so being in shape and displaying good racquet skills will definitely improve your credibility and self-confidence. As a high performance coach, it is also very useful to be able to work out with your players. The better player you are, the longer you will be able to keep up with them.

But most importantly, your own struggles with the game will help you to empathize with your players and to teach them from experience. It is easier to succeed as a coach if you have lived through the developmental process – if you understand the frustrations of losing matches that you should have won, or the frustration of failing to improve as fast as you would have liked to, or the anxiety of competition and the pain of conditioning.

The more you work on your own game, the better you will understand the game of tennis, and this experience will be invaluable to your students.

Keep hitting and keep learning!

PART V

Putting it all Together

You will learn: how to plan and manage your practices
to make the system more effective.

Training competitive players is not an exact science, and a coach has to adjust the length of these phases based on his players' schedule and ability. A phase can last for a month or for a day. For example, if my players start training in September to get ready for a competitive period in December, I could choose to have a preparation phase for six weeks, a pre-competitive phase for six weeks and a competitive phase for four weeks.

I could also select to run two cycles including all phases before the main competitive phase in December. Cycle one, September to October 15 and cycle two, October 16 to November 30. In this case each phase within a cycle would last a little less than two weeks.

Another option would be to treat each week as a cycle: Monday and Tuesday (general training phase), Wednesday and Thursday (pre-competitive phase), Friday and Saturday (competitive phase) Sunday (transition phase).

EG's COACHING WEAPONS

This is the art of coaching. There is no recipe to design the best training program for your players. However, thinking in terms of phases is very helpful. It provides guidance and a systematic approach to training.

Finally, it is very important to make sure the training plan addresses all aspects of the game. Within each training phase, strike a balance between work on groundstrokes and work on net play, between attacking and defending. Include serve and return and all the specialty shots. Working with a larger group, perhaps schedule on an alternate basis, one day groundstrokes and the next volleys or one day attacking game and the next defending game, etc.

When I was running the National Training Center in Mexico, we scheduled groundstroke practice on Monday, Wednesday and Friday, and volley practice on Tuesday and Thursday. That worked very well. On Tuesdays and Thursdays we would work on any area of the game that involved getting to the net: volleys, overheads, approach shots, serve and volley, return and volley, doubles, etc. The rest of the time the focus was more on the backcourt. It was a good way to develop complete players and add variety and fun to the practices.

Developing players is a science and an art.

SUMMARY
& CONCLUSIONS

You need to focus on different goals to develop better players: building flexible strokes, understanding the laws of the battle, incorporating these laws into your players' games, teaching your players how to move efficiently on the court, choosing an appropriate game style for your players, teaching your players how to deal with pressure and incorporating enough matches and competition to make it all work. The whole process is not sequential in nature so all the different skills have to be addressed simultaneously.

This chapter explained how to put everything together and how to plan your practices to make the system more effective. Thinking in terms of training phases and adjusting these phases based on your players' needs is the best way to implement all the developmental concepts.

Deliberate practice leads to success.

Enjoy the Process

High performance coaching is a very emotional endeavor with constant ups and downs. Just when you think everything is going well, and all your players are performing fine, disaster is only one tournament away. Bad losses, an injury, an illness, a personal problem, a bad day or a loss of motivation are only a few of the common events that will negatively affect your players and turn all your plans upside down.

During my term as a National Coach in Germany, there were three girls who reached the finals of the European Championships under fourteen or under sixteen and were not playing tennis at seventeen due to illness or burnout. And those were not isolated events; I witnessed many similar cases throughout my career.

Yet, tough times will also fade when you least expect it. Sometimes, a good match is all it takes to get a player back on track.

A great example of this is Vince Spadea, part of the first group of players in the USTA National Junior Team, traveling with me to Australia.

Vince broke into the top 20 on the ATP Tour in 1999 and got as high as 19 in the world that year. After that, he went through the biggest losing streak in the history of professional tennis, and his ranking dropped to 237.

Most people would have given up at that point, but Vince kept working, and finally, after 21 first round losses, he broke the streak at Wimbledon, beating Greg Rusedski on opening day 6-3, 6-7 (5), 6-3, 6-7 (8), 9-7. From that day, Vince started climbing up the rankings again, and in 2005 reached his highest career ranking of 18. This is an amazing feat and an admirable example of perseverance.

A player's career is totally unpredictable and so is the world of competitive coaching. It is a roller coaster ride with exhilarating ups and crushing downs, but knowing this will help you keep things in perspective.

Enjoy your work, and do not take wins or loses too seriously; both are just part of the process.

"Do not achieve to be happy but happily achieve."

FINAL NOTE

There you have it, a complete player development program with a clear structure, full of drills and ideas. However, there is one more thing that I would like to stress because of its extreme importance in player development. All the best drills in the world do not make a player. To become a great player you need to play as much as possible. After all it is called "playing tennis" not "drilling tennis."

To develop as a player you need to spend at least half of your court time playing sets, matches and tournaments. That is where you learn to put everything together, and where you are able to check your progress and make the necessary adjustments to your training schedule.

Although most responses are automatic once the ball is in play, the game does have an important strategic component that needs to be mastered as well. The goal of this book was to help develop players who will understand and play according to some important rules inherent in the game. Equally important is that they learn how to adjust slightly their game according to the opponent (strategy). For example: playing against a very weak backhand may alter the basic tactic of approaching the net down the line to exploit a weakness. A surprise change-up in tactics on key points might mean winning a vital game. Chipping and charging short crosscourt at 4-4, 30-40 is a good example.

These slight changes to the basic tactical concepts, so important to succeed, can only be learned through match experience. In addition, only through playing matches will you learn to deal with the pressure of competition, and competitive pressure is very hard to duplicate in practice. Using pressure drills will help, but it is not quite the same. Take ample opportunity to play practice matches and tournaments.

EG's COACHING WEAPONS

If I had to choose between two methods of developing players, one based on either drilling or playing a 100 percent of the time, I have no doubt that playing 100 percent of the time will produce better players.

I wanted to leave this point for the end of the book because it is essential to make the system work. Now, too many young players only set a foot on the court when participating in a formal lesson or training session and end up becoming champion drillers, not champion players.

Drilling is great, smart drilling is better, but lots of match play is essential. And here, I want to emphasize that when playing, variety is important. Teach your players to play against everyone and play everything: singles, doubles and mixed. Especially important, help your players understand that they should seek the opportunity to play against opponents whom they hate to play against, as often as possible. They are the ones who will challenge them to improve. Encourage them to play against them and deal with their uncomfortable game styles. It is human nature to "hate" that which we need the most. Overweight people hate to diet, stiff people hate to stretch, flunking students hate to study, and tennis players hate to play uncomfortable opponents. Players should compete against anyone to improve!

Too often I hear parents and students demanding to play against better players because they are the only ones who will "help" them develop their games. That is nonsense since playing all kinds of players is how one gets better. Playing better players is comfortable, because one does not have to face any pressure. One can play relaxed and not worry about losing. The real growth comes when facing the possibility of losing to someone who, in your mind, should not beat you.

Great champions are open to all challenges and use every opportunity to play and improve. If the adversary is far weaker, they will improve by trying to beat him with their weaknesses, polishing their own skills. Also a weaker opponent provides a great opportunity to work on the mental game by trying to win every single point.

If the opponent is at their level, they will try to embrace the battle and do everything they can to win. If the opponent is better, they will work hard to play every point to the best of their ability regardless of the score. It is a great opportunity to discover where their weaknesses are by analyzing how the opponent is able to counter their shots.

This reminds me of a little story many years ago when I took the U.S. National Junior Team to play tournaments in Europe.

Justin Gimelstob, a top ranked junior in the 90's, played an Austrian player named Stefan Koubek in an international junior tournament in Milan and got killed, leaving the court utterly frustrated. After he cooled off, and we got a chance to talk, I remember telling him to make sure to thank Stefan next time he saw him for pointing out how easy it was to attack his weak second serve! Stefan did a great job at the time, exploiting Justin's weakness and sending a clear message: "Either you improve your second serve, or you will face more pain in the future." Justin's serve improved quite a bit allowing him to become a very solid, top hundred professional player.

Play, play, play and learn from all your experiences!

No competition.....no players!

SUMMARY
& CONCLUSIONS

We can conclude the main section of this book by summarizing our player development system as follows:

1. Identify and practice all the different stroke variations that can be used in the game (technical flexibility).
2. Help the players master all of these different shot variations by constantly practicing them in drills as well as working on racquet head acceleration (technical flexibility).
3. Establish your laws of the battle.
4. Teach the players the laws of the battle, the different game styles and the concept of geometry of the court (tactical knowledge).
5. Incorporate all these concepts into their games by using feeding drills, standard response drills and guided tactical drills (automatic tactical responses).
6. Use movement training as an integral part of the program, on and off the court.
7. Help your players deal with stress by using pressure drills (tactical mastery).
8. Provide players plenty of opportunity to play, play, and play!!! (match toughness).

Tennis is a game for life. It is challenging, exciting and fun. At this point in the book I have finished my explanation of the player development system that I propose. The final two sections are meant to help you incorporate the system into your teaching. Section 13 lists **all** the laws of the battle that I use as a tactical blueprint, and section 14 is the Drill Library and includes **all** the drills mentioned in each chapter as well as a myriad of other drills that have worked for me in the past and that you can use to supplement your training program.

I hope this book has helped you understand the game better and made you a better coach or player.

Great Coaching is only Part of the Equation

It is important to understand that in player development, you, as a coach, are only one part of the equation. Several other aspects are just as important in the formation of players.

After working as a National Coach for the USA and Germany, I returned to Mexico to help their national player development program. Mexico has had some success in international tennis, with Rafael Osuna and Raul Ramirez, who were two of the top players in the world in their respective eras. After them, four or five players were ranked in the top 50 in the world, but that was more than two decades ago. Since then, Mexico has not had any top 100 player in singles. So, my job was to help devise a plan to develop a top 100 player in the near future.

Compared to the U.S. and Germany, where I had worked before, Mexico has extremely few resources devoted to sports in general, and tennis is no exception. Therefore, with a very limited budget, I had to devise a feasable plan, so I came up with the idea to start a self-sufficient National Training Center. It was basically a tennis academy where players would pay to train there, and sponsorship funds would be used to give scholarships and help pay for travelling expenses for our top players.

Mexico is a big country with a limited number of players. Most good players are isolated and have a hard time finding challenging competition where they live, so getting them together was a good way to help their development.

I was able to raise $100,000 US per year and ran the center for six years, until we ran out of money. We were able to support about 20 of our top juniors in the Training Center and started four or five schools in different parts of Mexico, where we were training about 400 players using a standarized system we developed. The players at the center would go to school in the mornings and practice for four hours in the afternoons. We were also able to form groups and travel around the world on the ITF circuit.

During those six years, three of our players reached a top 50 junior world ranking, and most of them ended up with a college scholarship in the U.S. There are still a few on the ATP circuit with one of them ranked in the 200's in doubles. It was a good effort, and I consider the project a success. However, we were far from being able to form a top 100 player, even though the quality of training we were providing was similar to that found in many of the top academies and national training centers around the world.

Good coaching is very important to develop players but there is a lot more to it. Without a large base of players, competition, resources to travel internationally and total support from the families, among other things, developing a world class player is extremely difficult. Moreover, even with all these factors in place, it is never easy. Just look at a country like England. They have spent millions of pounds in the last 25 years in their player development program, building facilities, training coaches, recruiting the best coaches in the world for their program, financially supporting their best players, and up to this point have only achieved limited results.

It has been a massive undertaking, and I am sure they will have a few top players in the future, but so far, the process has been painfully slow. On the other hand countries like Serbia or Belgium, with a small population and limited resources have been immensely successful in the last decade.

This brings us to one aspect that cannot be overlooked: "The Natural Order," a term I use to describe the fact that every person has different ability levels in any endeavour, and that in any group of people there is always going to be a natural-ability ranking for any activity.

The following hypothetical situation will help clarify this:

If you had unlimited resources and the capacity to recruit the 100 best prospects in the world to train them together at an academy, and you were also able to individualize each program to provide exactly what every player needed to reach his potential, after a few years you would have 100 great players, but also a number one and a number 100 in the group. Even in this small group, one player would be the best of the group and one would be the worst. That is just how it is. There is always going to be a natural order.

Coaching is only one part of the equation!

PART VI

Reference Library

This section is a complement to the coaching system.

Here you will find the laws of the battle that I use as my tactical blueprint, all the drills in the book and many other drills that I like as well as a glossary of important terms used throughout the book.

Laws of the Battle

In this section you will find my personal tactical blueprints for singles and doubles, the laws of the battle. It is my advice on the game, the heart of my tactical teachings and a key aspect of my training system: Teaching your players how to use their weapons effectively.

Build your standard response drills and guided tactical drills around these laws.

Laws of the Battle – Singles

Laws of the Serve

First Serve

The goal of the first serve is to force the opponent to return a weak shot and gain control of the point.

The first serve needs to be a weapon, not just a preview of the second serve. Take advantage of having two serves and be aggressive with the first serve. Use it to force a weak return from your opponent and gain control of the point. You will not get very far in competitive tennis if you cannot control the points with your first serve. I would even go so far as to say that in the men's game a player who is not able to serve consistently over 115 miles per hour, will not last too long on the tour.

Adjust your serve so that you can get at least 50 percent of first serves in; shoot for 70 percent.
A bullet is only effective if it hits the target. Having a "huge serve" might scare the opponent in the warm up but will only help you win the match if you can hit it with consistency.

Look to move into the court to attack a short return after your first serve.
Remember that the goal of your first serve is to force a weak return from the opponent, so make sure that you are expecting a short ball. There is nothing worse than hitting a great serve that the opponent barely hits over the net and then not being ready to attack the second shot. Next time you watch a professional tennis match count how many points are won by the server with his second shot – many.

Vary the location, pace and spin. Use the serve to the body.

Even a very hard serve will not be very effective if it is hit to the same spot every time. The key to great serving is to keep the opponent guessing. Use different spins, speeds and targets.

The serve to the body is a great option that is not used enough. A good serve to the body is especially effective on key points against an opponent who has been returning very well.

Use the slice serve to hit wide or to the T.

A slice serve bounces away from the player. The additional spin allows you to land the serve closer to the net when serving wide, thus pulling the opponent farther off the court. This is an especially effective serve against players with extreme grips or left-handers.

Second Serve

The goal of the second serve is to keep the returner in a neutral position.

From the returner's perspective a second serve is an opportunity to attack. Your goal as a server is to make sure you do not start the point on the defensive. If the opponent is constantly able to attack your second serve, you should take the hint and start practicing more.

Serve mostly to the opponent's weakness.

A very important element of the second serve is placement. You should be able to force the opponent to return using his weaker shot, not allowing him to run around your serve and use his strength.

The goal of the second serve is to keep the opponent from attacking you and if you are not able to force him to return with his weaker shot, you will most likely start the point on the defensive.

Use the serve into the body against an opponent who is chipping and charging.

Many attacking players will try to use the opponent's second serve to get the net. To do this effectively, they need to start moving toward the net before the server makes contact with the ball, allowing them to meet the ball well inside the court.

Serving into the body will make a smooth transition to the net a good deal more difficult since the attacker will have to move away from the ball to hit it and will lose forward momentum in doing so.

Hit the second serve at the maximum speed at which you can make a 100 percent of them.

A double fault is one of the worst mistakes in tennis. Besides costing a player the point, it is a blow to his confidence. Nothing affects your confidence more than not being able to count on your second serve. You need to find the ideal balance between power and control. Remember the old saying: "A player is only as good as his second serve."

General Serving Laws

Serve and volley if the opponent stands more than five feet behind the baseline to return.

An opponent standing far from the baseline to return will make it easier for you to get closer to the net after the serve and allow you to hit a higher volley. The serve and the return will have to travel a longer distance, giving you more time to get to the net. Surprise the returner by coming in more often after your serve.

Serve and volley if the opponent keeps slicing the return.

A slice return is a control shot with little power. Serving and volleying against an opponent who slices the return will guarantee that you will get your racquet on the ball. The rest is up to you. This strategy is even more effective if you are able to surprise the opponent. In this case you will normally face a comfortable volley.

Serve mostly to your opponent's weakness but vary the placement and spin. A 25 percent variation is enough to keep him guessing.

You want to use your serve to gain control of the point. Serving to the weakness is a good strategy. However, keeping the opponent guessing will give you an added advantage. Changing one out of every four serves is enough to achieve this.

Serve to the weak side on key points.

Sometimes, tennis players have peculiar ways of thinking. When facing an opponent with a much weaker stroke they choose the key points to "surprise" him. I have seen this over and over. One of my players is playing a close match against an opponent with a much weaker backhand doing well serving there. Suddenly, at four all deuce he tries to "surprise" the opponent and serves to the forehand. The outcome is rarely pretty, and the only one surprised is the server when the return blasts past him. You have to learn to play the odds. If the opponent has a weak shot, the last thing he wants is to use it on big points. Use serve change-ups at the beginning of the game or when you are comfortably up, but not on key points.

Most important shot...less practiced shot.

Laws of the Battle

Focus on the contact point when under pressure or when you feel your serve is off.

Most players are aware of the importance of watching the ball when hitting groundstrokes or volleys but do not think it applies to the serve.

EG's COACHING WEAPONS

Achieving an optimal contact point is the key to hitting a solid shot, and the serve is no exception. All body segments need to be coordinated to achieve an optimal contact point and the only way to do this effectively is by watching the ball all the way until contact.

The most common mistake when serving, especially under pressure, is pulling the head down too early.

Try to stretch the opponent with your serve.

Balance is the key to returning well. A well placed serve that stretches the opponent is more effective than a hard serve that can be returned in balance without much body movement.

Work on being able to hit the slice and the flat serve in different directions off the same toss.

On the professional circuit, the time that a player has to react to return serve is often less than the time it takes for the opponent's serve to reach him. The returner has to start moving before the server makes contact with the ball. This can only be accomplished if the returner is able to pick up specific clues from the server before he makes contact with the ball such as the position of the ball toss. Therefore, a good server has to be able to vary the serve's position and spin using the same toss. Practice, by having someone tell you where to hit the serve after you have tossed the ball (body, T or wide).

Run to the net following the direction of your serve when you serve and volley.

Based on the geometry of the court, we know that the ideal position at the net varies and depends on the placement of the approach shot or volley. A shot to the right requires a position at the net to the right of the center and vice versa. The same concept applies to serving and volleying. The best position following a serve to the middle is toward the middle, and the best position at the net following a wide serve is toward the side of the serve. Following the ball when running toward the net is an easy way to reach the ideal position every time.

Use the slice serve to the body if the opponent is returning very well.

Many players, especially tall ones, need some space to hit the ball well and are used to moving laterally to return. Surprise them with a serve into the body.

Make sure you get the first serve in after a double fault.

Nothing leaves you more vulnerable as a player than double faulting. If you miss the first serve after a double fault, you face a zero for three count, which will greatly increase the probability of double faulting again. To avoid this uncomfortable situation, after a double fault hit the first serve as if it were a second serve.

LAWS OF THE RETURN

First Serve Return

Return down the middle of the court or crosscourt.

When returning a first serve, it is easy to be late at contact due to the speed of the ball. Aiming at the middle of the court or crosscourt will give you a better chance of making the return. If you are late at contact, your ball will fade down the line but will still land inside the court. If you aim down the line, a late contact point will produce a sideline mistake.

Use slice if you are going to block the return.

When you are blocking a return, your goal is to make the opponent play. However, you need to make sure that the opponent is not able to attack you. If you block the return with topspin and it lands short, the opponent will have an easy shoulder level shot. If you block the return with slice and it lands short, the opponent will have a harder time attacking it since the ball will stay low.

Keep the return deep. Strive to start the point in a neutral position.

The goal of the server is to use his first serve to force a weak return. The goal of the returner is a neutral shot to avoid being on the defensive. Focus on keeping the ball deep as opposed to hitting harder.

Second Serve Return

Go down the line if you can hurt the opponent, otherwise down the middle or crosscourt.

If you return down the line without hurting the opponent, you will leave yourself vulnerable to an aggressive crosscourt shot that will put you on the defensive. If you are not able to hurt the opponent, return down the middle or crosscourt to keep yourself in a better position to start the rally.

Laws of the Battle

Adjust where you stand to return second serves. Look to use your weapon and move into the court to catch the ball early.

A second serve is a great opportunity to attack. Moving into the court to return puts you in a better position to return aggressively. In addition, make sure you take advantage of a slow second serve and move around to use your best shot. This can be done in two ways: Move in before the opponent serves if you want the opponent to see you and start thinking about it. Hopefully he will second-guess himself. Or, move as he tosses if you want to surprise him.

I have won many important points in my career by waiting for a 30/40 and second serve situation on a key game in a match and moving to the alley inside the court before the opponent's second serve. Quite often, the opponent will double fault. Changing your position on the court at this key moment forces the opponent to rethink, and that is usually enough to force a double fault.

Move diagonally toward the ball to catch it early if the opponent is using kick serves. Do not let the ball get above your shoulders.

It is very difficult to hit a solid return when contacting the ball above the shoulders. Moving into the court and contacting the ball before it gets above the shoulders is the best way to counter a good kick serve.

Attack a weak second serve!

Strive to control the point with the return against a weak serve.

One of the basic tactical concepts of the game is to hit the ball deep until you get a short ball from the opponent, which you can attack. In many cases, the second serve is the first short ball that you get in the point. Do not let the opportunity to attack go by; be aggressive.

If you run around the backhand on the ad court, use an inside out forehand unless you are going for a winner.

When running around the backhand to hit a forehand from the ad court, you will get yourself near or on the alley and out of position since you will be hitting from the backhand side of the court. Hitting the forehand inside in (down the line) will leave you vulnerable to a good crosscourt shot from the opponent. Start your attack with an inside out forehand and repeat that shot until you are in control of the point. Use the inside in sparingly to keep the opponent out of balance.

Return wide serves crosscourt or down the middle. Only go down the line if you are going for a winner.

Wide serves will take you off the court. As you know from the geometry of the court, hitting crosscourt will keep you closer to the "ideal" court position. If you return down the line and are not able to hurt the opponent, you will be left vulnerable to a crosscourt shot that will easily put you on the defensive. Therefore, if you decide to go down the line be very aggressive and try to hurt the opponent.

Chip & Charge

Start moving forward as the opponent tosses the ball.

A common mistake players make when chipping and charging is waiting for the ball, hitting the return, and then moving toward the net. To chip and charge effectively, you need to contact the ball early while moving toward the net. To accomplish this, you need to start moving forward when the opponent tosses to serve. Split step as the opponent makes contact and continue moving toward the incoming ball. Make contact with the ball in front of you and continue moving toward the net, keeping this whole process as fluid as possible. The goal is for you to get close to the net to hit your first volley.

On the ad court always try using your backhand when chipping and charging. On the deuce court always try to use your forehand (right-handed player).

When chipping and charging it is very important to cover the court effectively after the return. Your goal should be to use the stroke that leaves you in the best possible position after the return.

For a right-handed player, using the forehand on the deuce court and the backhand on the ad court will accomplish this by allowing you to remain near the center of the court.

A common mistake is running around the backhand on the ad court, thus leaving the whole court open.

Play to the middle of the court or down the line unless you can hurt the opponent.
Playing the return crosscourt and coming in will leave you vulnerable to a down the line passing shot since you will probably not have the time to reach the ideal position at the net before the opponent makes contact with the ball. For this reason you should only chip and charge crosscourt if you can hurt the opponent by getting him out of balance or forcing him to try to pass you with his weaker shot.

Clay Court Return:
Use a longer swing with good acceleration and hit higher over the net.
On a hard court, blocking the ball with compact swings is a very effective return of serve tactic. This strategy will not work very well on a clay court. A clay court will slow down the ball and make it bounce higher. Using very compact strokes to return will normally lead to short returns that can be attacked. A good alternative to try on clay is to take advantage of a slower bounce and use a bigger swing to return a heavier ball.

Move farther back to return.
The basic return strategy on a hard court is to step toward the ball and block the return with a very short swing using the speed of the incoming serve. On a clay court this strategy sometimes backfires because a blocked return that is not hit very deeply tends to sit up on the slow surface giving the opponent an easy shot to attack.

A good alternative on a slow court is to take advantage of a slower bouncing serve to move back and take a full swing at the ball. Most good clay court players on the professional tour use this strategy.

General Laws of the Return
Always make the opponent play.
The return is your first shot in the point. It is imperative that you put the ball in the court and get the point started. Before trying anything else, make sure that you are making the opponent play with consistent returns of serve.

Vary your position to adjust to the server. Cover his favorite shot.

You need to remember that you can stand anywhere you want to return. If you are not being successful in your usual position, move around and try to find the ideal position against the opponent you are facing. Adjust your position based on your opponent's patterns and the score. Example: If the opponent serves very well wide, stand closer to the sidelines, especially on key points.

This point reminds me of a junior I used to coach. He was playing an ITF tournament against a strong Japanese player who had a wonderful slice serve that kept acing him wide on the deuce court. After the match, I asked my player why he did not adjust his stance to cover the wide serve. All he had to do was to stand closer to the sideline and challenge his opponent to serve down the T, a serve that he rarely used. This is what he responded: "But coach, he kept surprising me to the forehand." From then on our inside joke was to remind him not to be "surprised" over and over by the same shot.

Move in to return a kick serve.

Laws of the Battle

The way I try to explain similar situations to my players is as follows: If someone hits a shot that you are not expecting, blame it on surprise. If someone "surprises" you again with exactly the same shot, the word you are looking to describe that situation is stupidity, not surprise.

On key points, return the first serve FH to FH and BH to BH or to the middle.

This is a tactical concept that I learned from Tom Gullikson, former USA Davis Cup team captain.

On key points you want to give yourself the best chance of making the opponent play. When returning a first serve it is easy to hit the return late. If you aim down the line, any late hit will result in a lateral mistake. However, by aiming at the middle or crosscourt (forehand to forehand or backhand to backhand) any late hit will result in a shot bouncing in the middle of the court or down the line.

Put pressure on the server by varying your position on key points.

Servers get used to seeing you in the same spot every time they serve. Letting your opponents see you in a different spot, either closer to the service line, favoring your best shot or covering their favorite serve, will automatically increase the pressure on them.

Using this strategy sparingly and mainly on key points is extremely effective and can earn you many important points through double faults.

Rafael Osuna, the great Mexican player of the 60's, used this strategy very effectively. He was known for standing very close to the service line against some of the fastest servers of his generation. This usually led to erratic serving by his opponents, who were trying to serve harder than normal in response to his bravado.

Do not let the opponent surprise you with his favorite serve on key points.

Every player has a favorite serve, and players tend to use their favorite serves when under pressure or when facing a very important point. Throughout the match, be aware of your opponent's tendencies and try to keep them in mind. Make sure you are ready to cover them on key points.

Complete focus!

Against a serve and volleyer, hit at his feet to the middle of the court on first serves. Make the volleyer stretch on second serve returns.

Aiming at the middle of the court on first serve returns helps improve the consistency of your returns. First serves are fast and easy to hit late. Aiming too close to the lines will lead to unforced errors.

On second serve returns, it is easier to achieve an ideal contact point and therefore to place the ball where you want it. Stretching a serve and volleyer will force mistakes.

Stay relaxed and watch the ball after the bounce.

The two most common causes of mistakes in the return are not watching the ball and tensing up. This is something that I can really relate to because it affected me for a long time. Growing up, I went through a period of time when I could not return. I was playing well in general, but I was missing too many returns. After much tinkering and trying different approaches, I finally realized that I was not able to track the ball to contact. I was tensing up and was losing the ball after the bounce. Of course, I had no idea I was tensing up because I had been doing it for so long that I could not even feel it. However, once I was aware of it and started working on staying relaxed through the shot and tracking the ball from the bounce to the racquet, everything fell into place. I suddenly developed into a competent returner.

RALLYING LAWS

Play consistently; do not beat yourself.

EG's COACHING WEAPONS

The hardest shot will not win you points if it does not land in the court. Play aggressively but at a speed that you can control. Ask yourself on the changeover: Am I losing on my mistakes or is the opponent beating me? Your goal should be to make sure the opponent beats you by his skill and not your errors.

Play neutral or lifting shots mainly crosscourt.

Adjust your swing to the incoming ball (short backswing for off the bounce shots, dipping shots and against short and low balls).

A common mistake is to try to swing the same way at every ball, which will lead to very inconsistent play. Every shot has different characteristics and should be handled accordingly. In general, use long swings against very slow balls or when hitting from far behind the baseline. Use short backswings when the balls are coming fast or very deep and when you find yourself close to the net or facing a very short, low ball.

Play neutral and lifting shots mainly crosscourt.

As we learned from our discussion of the geometry of the court, playing crosscourt keeps you closer to the ideal court position after the shot. When you play down the line, the ideal court position after the shot is farther away making it harder to cover the court effectively. Unless you can hurt the opponent, play the shot crosscourt.

Use down the line shots when you are inside the baseline and can hurt the opponent.

Hitting down the line makes it harder to reach the ideal court position to cover the opponent's next shot, so use the down the line shots only when you can hurt the opponent. If the opponent is out of balance, he will not be able to hurt you even if you are not in the ideal position to cover the court.

Use angles when you are in an attacking position inside the baseline. Try to move the opponent outside the singles lines.

A short ball from the opponent is the ideal situation to use a crosscourt dipping shot to force the opponent to move outside the singles sidelines and open the court. Trying to hit an angle while behind the baseline will not be very effective since it will usually not force the opponent off the court and can be risky.

Laws of the Battle

When you are in a defensive position and out of balance, hit high (lifting shot) crosscourt or to the center of the court.

Balance is a key element in the game, and tennis is really a battle for balance. The player who can stay in balance the most during a match will normally win. Hitting a high deep ball when out of balance will give you a better chance to stay in the point and more time to get back to the ideal court position before the opponent hits the next shot. Hitting crosscourt or down the middle will provide you with the best opportunity to regain balance and control of the point.

Use the lifting shot when you have to back up during your stroke.

Ideally, you should always strive to move forwards to hit the ball, but sometimes the opponent's shot will force you to move backwards to hit. In this situation do not try to hit a low aggressive shot since it is very difficult to hit from far behind the baseline while leaning backwards. Instead, hit a high aggressive shot, deep into the opponent's court.

Always try to step into the court and catch the ball early when you have the opponent in trouble.

Catching the ball early reduces the amount of time the opponent has to move toward the middle of the court after his last shot and therefore gives him less time to cover the next shot. Good players have learned to recognize situations when their opponent is in trouble, which may lead to short or high balls. When this happens, they always move forward looking to catch the ball early to continue their attack.

As a National Coach for the German Federation, I was coaching their top junior girls who were trying to make the transition from the juniors to the pros. One of the skills that we practiced over and over was to move into the court after hitting an aggressive shot and strive to catch the next ball early, even out of the air when possible. Invariably, when the junior girls started playing against the pros, the first thing they realized was how much better the pros defended. They did a much better job making the opponent play additional shots even when the point was already almost lost. They were very skillful at hitting high defensive shots when totally out of position. The young girls, not used to this, lost many points after having the opponent "on the ropes," by letting a high defensive shot bounce and giving the opponents enough time to regain balance.

If you run around the backhand, always start the attack with an inside out forehand. Do not go down the line with the forehand until you are in control of the point.

Running around the backhand will position you close to the sideline. Playing the shot down the line to the opponent's forehand (assuming both players are right handed) leaves you out of position to cover a crosscourt shot to the open court. When running around the forehand, start the attack inside out to the opponent's backhand and wait for a short ball to go down the line.

Use a drop shot only when you are in control of the point and inside the court. Use disguise.
A drop shot is only effective when you are able to surprise the opponent. The best way to surprise the opponent is to hit it when inside the court in an aggressive position. The opponent will be expecting a hard deep shot and will have little time to react. If you try to hit a drop shot from behind the baseline, the shot will be much harder to execute, and the opponent will have more time to get to it.

Constantly look for opportunities to move into the court and catch the ball early. Move diagonally to the ball.
Catching the ball before it drops will give the opponent less time to get into the ideal position to cover the court. By moving diagonally to the ball instead of laterally you will constantly rush the opponent. Therefore, this should be one of the main goals for every player.

Vary the pace, height and spin of the rally to force a short shot from the opponent.
The more variation in your shots, the more likely your opponent will make a judgment mistake. Tennis is a game of coordination and in order to execute with consistency the player has to hit the ball at an ideal contact point. Slight variations in this contact point can lead to large variations in the trajectory of the ball. Different spins, heights and speeds will likely lead to more errors from your opponent.

LAWS OF THE ATTACKING GAME

Try to keep the ball deep and low when approaching the net.

Deep and low is better than hard and short when you are approaching the net. You want to keep the ball low to make the opponent hit up and allow you to hit a high volley. In addition you want to hit deep to have as much time as possible to move to the ball at the net. A good strategy is to use slice when attacking low short balls to help you keep the ball low.

Approach mainly to the weaker side or down the line when you cannot hurt the opponent.

No one likes to try to hit a passing shot with a stroke that does not feel very comfortable, so approaching to your opponent's weaker side should be your first strategy. If both sides are about the same, approach down the line to be able to cover the court better as we learned in our discussion of the geometry of the court.

Use approach shots to the center of the court if your opponent hits good angles.

Players with good passing shots usually move well and hit good angles. An approach down the center of the court takes the opponent's angle option away and usually allows the player approaching a chance to volley.

Be decisive and intense when moving forward.

When approaching the net, hit crosscourt to the open court only if you can hurt the opponent with an off the shoulder shot inside the baseline.

As discussed earlier, approaching down the line leaves you in a better position to cover the court. Therefore, only hit the approach shot crosscourt when you can hurt the opponent with your shot.

Surprise the opponent by attacking the net at the last second when you have him outstretched or when he is moving back to return a high deep shot.

Once you have the opponent stretched, he will very likely play a defensive shot. Staying at the baseline and letting the ball bounce will only let him back into the point. Do not miss the opportunity to keep the opponent on the defensive by running to the net and catching the ball out of the air to force the opponent with the next shot. Do this even when you did not plan to move in before you hit the shot. As soon as you see the opponent stretched and in a defensive position, move in and surprise him.

Follow the path of the ball when coming in. Do not move to the middle of the court every time.

Your ideal position at the net depends on the direction of your approach shot. Running to the net following the direction of this shot is a good way to end up in the ideal court position at the net (left from the center line when approaching to the left side of the court and right from the center line when approaching to the right side of the court).

Always recover quickly following your shot after each volley.

When at the net you do not have very much time between your volley and the opponent's passing shot so it is very important that you use every second by moving in the direction of your volley as soon as you hit it.

EG's COACHING WEAPONS

"Hit and recover and you will clobber, hit and stay and you will pay."

Long lobs should be countered by deep overheads; short lobs should be angled off.

When facing a deep lob aim your overhead safely, so that it bounces toward the baseline. When facing a short lob, angle it off trying to bounce it toward the sidelines to finish the point.

Laws of the Battle

When you attack the net with an inside out forehand cover the down the line passing shot.

By running around the backhand to approach with an inside out forehand, you will usually hit the ball from the backhand side of the court with the same trajectory as a crosscourt backhand approach, leaving the right side of the court vulnerable for a down the line pass. If you hit a solid inside out shot, you will stretch the opponent, and from a stretched position it will be easier to hit down the line, so make sure you are ready for that shot.

Play the high volley firmly to the open court.

Playing a volley crosscourt may leave you out of position for the next shot. However, if you are faced with a high volley, playing it firmly crosscourt is an excellent way to finish the point or, at the very least, force the opponent.

Play the low volleys deep down the line or hit a drop shot.

It will be more difficult to force the opponent with a low volley so you want to make sure that you are in good position for the next shot. Play the volley to the opponent's weakness if there is a clear difference between his forehand and backhand. If both sides are equal, play down the line to maintain good court position. Hit a drop volley as a variation, but use it sparingly.

Play half volleys deep and consistently. Do not try to hit a great shot if you are in a defensive position. Your goal is to make the opponent pass you.

Many times when approaching the net, you will be faced with a good shot from the opponent that will force you to hit a half volley. Under these circumstances the tendency is to panic and try to hit a great shot to get back on the offensive. However, this usually leads to unforced errors. When facing a half volley, remain calm and recognize that your opponent has put you in a less offensive situation. Play a deep shot and force the opponent to hit another passing shot. You will be amazed how many more points you win by giving the opponent another chance to miss.

When stretched at the net, hit a drop volley or deep down the line. Only go crosscourt if you can hurt the opponent.

A ball that stretches you at the net will pull you off the court, making it harder to cover the next shot. If you go crosscourt, you need to make sure that you are able to force the opponent, or you will not be able to cover the down the line passing shot. If you find yourself stretched and in no position to hit an aggressive volley, volley down the line or hit a down the line drop shot.

Look for depth when stretched at the net.

When serving and volleying, serve to the T on key points to avoid opening the court to angles.
Wide serves will allow the opponent to use more angles on the return. Serving to the T will make it easier to cover the return. Having said that, if the opponent has a much weaker side, serve to that side on key points.

Use short, low slice approaches as a variation against very good passers.
Sometimes a short, low, slice approach will force the opponent to hit up on his passing shot, making it easier to volley. Since the opponent will be inside the court, he will not be able to hit the low ball too hard, or it will fly out. Use this shot as a variation or against players who are not able to hit the ball with much topspin.

LAWS OF THE PASSING GAME

Make the opponent play. Do not try to pass on the first shot (unless the opponent leaves the court wide open).

EG's COACHING WEAPONS

"The best way to hit a passing shot is not to hit a passing shot."

One of the most common mistakes when facing an opponent charging the net is to panic and try to hit a super untouchable shot. Doing this will lead to more mistakes than great shots and is therefore counterproductive. When the opponent charges the net, think about hitting a low shot to force the opponent to volley up. Then look for the next shot to pass him. By making the opponent volley up you raise the odds of winning the point considerably. First there is a chance that the opponent will miss the volley, and second if you kept the ball low, his volley will most likely allow you to hit a comfortable second shot.

Catch the ball early when hitting a passing shot. Move toward the ball if possible.
Catching the ball early will give the opponent less time to get close to the net and therefore less time to get into a good position to cover the net. By quickly moving toward the ball when facing an approach shot, you will increase your chances of stretching the opponent at the net and forcing him to hit a weak volley that will leave you in a good position to win the point.

After a passing shot, move diagonally into the court looking to catch the volley early.
One of the most important elements when trying to pass an opponent is to hit the passing shot and move diagonally into the court. This allows you to catch the next shot early and reduce the amount of time the opponent has to cover your passing shot. Too many players hit a passing shot and remain behind the baseline waiting for the opponent to volley. In most cases they are beaten by a short volley, and in the best of cases the volleyer remains in control of the point and ends up winning it after a couple of volleys.

Dipping shots will force the volleyer to hit up.

It is important to understand that a volleyer will volley short rather than deep. It is much harder to volley deep, especially when stretched or when facing a very low ball. The passer should be anticipating the most likely scenario, a short ball, and move into the court following the passing shot.

Use a dipping shot or an off the bounce shot, making the opponent volley.
When facing an approach shot you will normally have two options. If the approach shot is short you should use a dipping shot with a lot of spin to force the opponent to volley up. If the opponent's approach shot is deep, catch the ball early by using an off the bounce shot to reduce the time the opponent has to get to the net.

Use lobs to force the opponent to stand farther back at the net.
The lob is a key tool for any good passer. Playing really close to the net will give the volleyer a great advantage in terms of court coverage since the closer to the net, the easier it is to cover the angles. For this reason, it is important to make sure the opponent is not able to get too close to the net. A lob is a great weapon to keep him guessing and off the top of the net.

Use a high defensive lob when on the run and not able to take a good swing at the ball. Use the same shot when having been passed by a lob.
If you find yourself stretched and with no chance of executing a decent swing give yourself another chance to get back in the point by playing a high, deep lob. The same shot will keep you in the point when you are running back to retrieve a lob that went over your head.
Make sure your lob is very high. There are no lines in the sky.

Stay relaxed and watch the ball at contact. Most passing shot errors are due to tension or lack of focus on the ball.
A passing shot is a situation of great pressure. It is very easy to get distracted and anxious by the opponent charging the net. Under these circumstances don't miss the shot by being tentative or by not focusing on the ball at contact. To improve your chances of making the shot, decide early where you will hit the shot, stay relaxed and focus on the contact point, not on the opponent or on your target.

Use a low slice at the opponent's feet or a lob if the opponent stretches you, and you are not able to take a good swing at the ball.

Trying to hit a passing shot when out of balance and stretched will most likely lead to a mistake. Give yourself a chance to stay in the point by keeping the ball low with slice or hitting a lob.

Hit mostly crosscourt passing shots on key points to leave the opponent without an angle and guarantee a second opportunity to pass.

Hitting a passing shot down the line will allow the opponent to hit an angle volley that will keep the ball moving away from you over the sideline, making it more difficult to reach. By hitting your passing shot crosscourt, you are hitting over the lowest part of the net, and the opponent's down the line volley to the open court will travel parallel to the sideline, giving you a better opportunity to reach it.

Play a deep shot down the line in response to a drop shot unless you can get there early and attack the shot crosscourt.

When facing a drop shot it is very tempting to hit crosscourt away from the opponent. However, if the drop shot forces you, you will most likely face a low shot and will not be able to force the opponent. In this case, going crosscourt will only leave you vulnerable to a down the line passing shot. Keep the ball down the line and deep after running down a drop shot. Now you are in the best possible position to cover the opponent's next shot. Only play crosscourt when you get to the shot early and can play more offensively.

If you can return an opponent's overhead, make sure you make him play. Do not go for the winner; you are back in the point.

After hitting a lob, you are usually in a defensive position. Being able to return an overhead is a great momentum changer. The opponent thinks he has the point, and suddenly he has to keep fighting for it. Frequently, there is an urge to play a great shot after reaching the opponent's overhead. Resist that urge and make sure the opponent plays the next shot. Keep the ball low or hit another lob to the backhand. You will have a much better chance of winning the point just by making the opponent play as opposed to going for a winner.

LAWS OF MATCH PLAY

During the warm up, focus on swinging relaxed and watching the ball, especially after it bounces and all the way to the contact point.

Good players use the warm up to prepare mentally and physically for the match. Before a tournament match most players are nervous and tend to fill their minds with anxious thoughts and ideas: How good is this player? I should win this match; he doesn't look very tough, etc. Focusing solely on the ball will help you keep your mind on the task at hand and will set a good mental base for the competition.

Do not beat yourself. If you lose make sure the opponent has beaten you.

EG's COACHING WEAPONS

The most important two rules in tennis are:
Hit the ball over the net and hit the ball within the lines.

Set a solid base at the start of a match.

It is surprising to see how easily people forget these simple rules. Too many times, players are so focused on trying to beat the opponent with great shots that they forget to hit the ball in the court. By the time the match ends the opponent did not have to do anything to win except duck a few times to avoid the fence-seeking "missiles."

Before trying to beat the opponent with clean winners, test his ability by hitting at a pace at which you are comfortable. In other words, play your game first and adjust if necessary.

Set a good base at the start of the match.
At the beginning of the match you have to focus on the following aspects:
>> Make all the returns. Play them safely to the middle of the court.
>> Use spin on your first serve to make a high percentage of them.
>> Play mostly neutral shots crosscourt off the ground to get rhythm and to discover what the opponent can and cannot do.

At the start of a match everyone is nervous so the chances to miss are greater. Playing solidly at the beginning will allow you to relax and to test the opponent. If you are nervous and try to play too well from the beginning, chances are that you will make mistakes and become even more nervous. On the other hand, if you make the opponent play at first, you can always play more aggressively if you have to, once you relax.

It is amazing how many more matches one can win when one lets the opponent make mistakes.

Try to keep your shots deep and make sure you are not missing into the net.
A common mistake is to aim very close to the net especially when hitting hard or attacking, causing many mistakes. Experienced players on the other hand, play high over the net and use spin to keep the ball in the court no matter how hard they hit. A good strategy, in general, is to aim at least two feet over the net on every groundstroke. Not only will you cut down your mistakes, but also, your balls will be more effective by landing deeper in the court.

Play your strengths. Once you establish a solid base try to impose your game style on the opponent.
Your first strategy should always be to feel comfortable on the court by playing mainly the shots you like to play. Then you will gain confidence and force the opponent to play on your terms. It is difficult to be a master of all trades. Every player has certain shots and patterns that he likes most.

Everyone has favorite patterns.

Build your game around these strengths and adjust it slightly according to the opponent's game. For example, if you like to come to the net, play your match that way but adjust your approach shots based on the opponent's strengths and weaknesses.

You will never see Nadal, the master of clay court tennis, become a net rusher at Wimbledon. He may serve and volley a little more and come to the net a few more times, but he will remain faithful to his basic patterns and game style.

Find the opponent's weaknesses and patterns.

Look for what the opponent can and can't do. Play to the opponent's weaknesses. In addition, pay attention to his common patterns of play. Make sure that you are aware of those patterns, especially during important points.

For example, if the opponent's favorite serve is wide, make sure you look for this serve. Even stand a bit closer to the side to cover his best serve more easily and force him to try a different serve.

EG'S COACHING WEAPONS

I have heard Wimbledon champion Stan Smith talk about this several times, and his explanation goes something like this: During the match you make a mental note of what is happening; what are your opponent's tendencies, what is he doing well and what can you exploit? Then wait for key points to capitalize on these tendencies. For example: If you are playing an opponent who is getting very close to the net when he attacks. Wait for a key point to lob. That one lob could decide the match.

Always try to close in at the net to hit the volley as close to the net as possible.

The closer to the net the more aggressive you can be, since you will be able to hit the ball at a higher point with a better chance of hitting down into the opponent's court. However, you have to find a balance between being close in and being able to cover the lob at the same time.

Fight to catch the lob in the air.

When at the net, always play to the baseline player unless you can hurt the opponent at the net. Play low volleys crosscourt towards the player in the back and high volleys down the line at the net player.

If you are at the net and have a volley that you can hit down with good speed, aim at the feet of your opponent at the net. If you face a low volley, aim at the opponent at the baseline. Do not volley to the opponent at the net unless you can hurt him. The same rule applies to short balls. Unless you can really drill a shot at the net person with consistency, it is better to play a safe shot to the opponent on the baseline and follow your shot to the net.

The problem with this law is that in the early stages of learning to play doubles, hitting towards the net person might not be a bad strategy because novice players are usually timid and not very good at the net. As the competition grows, playing to the net man from a defensive or neutral position will not win you many points.

Who covers the middle? The player standing diagonally to the incoming shot always covers the middle.

Every time I ask who covers the middle in doubles, I get the same response: The player with the forehand volley. When I ask: What happens if two lefties are playing or if one of the players has a much better backhand volley? They just look at me as though I have lost my mind. The forehand volley does not take the middle. That is an old wife's tale. It is impossible to think about who has the forehand in the middle of the point.

Going back to our discussion of the geometry of the court, a singles player should always place himself in the middle of the opponent's best possible shots in order to cover the court effectively. Doubles is no different, and a good doubles team will achieve this by always following their shot. Therefore, if a team hits a shot to the left side of the court, the team will move to the left. The player diagonal to the shot will move toward the middle and his partner toward the alley. "The player diagonal to the shot Always covers the middle."

When in doubt hit the ball between the opponents at the net.

Many times after a good return we become anxious about the next shot. Do not panic! You do not need to kill someone on the next shot. You do not even have to maim him. Give your opponents an extra opportunity to miss. Hit the second shot between the volleyers and be patient. You will be surprised at how many points you win if you consistently make the serving team play at least two shots per point.

Always look to hit at the opponents' feet. Low volleys should be hit with little pace at the opponents' feet, closing in after the shot.

Many times a low, softer shot will be more effective than a hard-hit volley. When facing a low volley with the opponents at the net, the tendency is to try to hit a firm volley through them. However, the shot that will win more points is a low, soft shot at their feet followed by a move forward to cut off their next shot. The opponents will have to hit up to clear the net and if you move fast toward the net, you should be left with a high volley to put away.

I learned this lesson back in college when I had to play Jorge Lozano and Todd Witsken from the University of Southern California, who later became the number one doubles team in the world. They had great feel for the ball. Every time we exchanged volleys at the net, they would slow down the ball and dump it to our feet. It was extremely uncomfortable, and, unfortunately for us, very effective for them.

Talk to your partner after every point.

Communication is the key for great doubles. Doubles is a team sport. You have to work together with your partner. Make sure you promote interaction with your partner by checking in with him after every point. There are many important aspects that you need to address to be on the same page, such as where to serve, cross or not cross, opponents' weaknesses, etc. Moreover, make sure you support your partner unconditionally, even after missing that 'sitter' at break point. Especially after missing that 'sitter'! Bite your tongue and use all of your inner strength to lie to him: "It does not matter."

Kidding aside, no one misses on purpose. Responding negatively to your partner's mistakes will just lead to more insecurity and errors.

Give directions to your partner during the point.

Doubles requires great communication, and it is advisable to talk to your partner as often as possible between points. However, communication during the point is just as important.

You and your partner should help each other out as much as possible on the court. Call out-balls aloud to your partner. Sometimes a player in a different court position is not able to judge the path of the ball as well as his partner. In addition, call "mine" for all the shots to the middle of the court that you want to take.

Another situation occurs when you are about to lob. Yelling "back" as you are about to hit the ball will give your partner extra time to back off into a defensive position in case your lob is short.

There may be other situations when and where you need your partner to move a certain way to cover the court better. Do not hesitate in guiding him during the point: stay, back, go, and so forth.

Always make the first serve against two players who stay back to receive.

In doubles you are in the best position to win the point when you are at the net. When the opponents decide to play both back when you serve, make sure you get the first serve in and run to the net. You really want to take advantage of the opportunity of playing two at the net against two at the baseline. Missing that first serve will usually give the opponents a reason to change the formation to one up one back, leaving your team in a weaker position.

When playing against two players who stay back, volley down the middle of the court unless you have a high volley that you can angle off. Keep volleying deep and wait for the lob.

If you get into the situation where you and your partner are at the net, and the opponents are both back, keep volleying deep, through the middle of the court, taking away any angles from the opponents. Do not give in to the temptation of hitting a drop shot or a "cute little angle" because if it is not perfect, you will open up the court and give the rivals an opportunity to attack. Keep volleying deep until you have a high volley or overhead to angle off.

If you decide to use the formation of both back to return, never miss the return.

One of the things that drives me crazy as a coach is to see both my players play back on the return and then just try to hit the same return that they would have hit if they were playing one up one back. That is insane; if you are planning to play an aggressive return, make sure your partner is at the net ready to back it up.

When you ask your partner to stay back while you return, what you are really telling him is "I do not feel very confident with my ability to hit an aggressive return to the opponent's feet. Please stay back so that we can play more defensively." Going for a huge return after this 'statement' is absurd. Get the return in any way you can, lob it, block it or dink it. Do whatever you want but do not miss it by going for a winner. Stay true to the logic behind the strategy of playing both back!

Use a High Lob to the middle of the court if you have to run back to chase a lob that you could not hit in the air.

If your team gets lobbed, and one of you has to run back to chase the lob, play a high defensive lob aiming at the middle of the court. This will give both of you time to get back to the baseline to play defense. Many players make the mistake of trying to hit an offensive shot from that position. Most of the time they will lose the point either by missing the shot or by giving the other team a high volley that will be put away.

When caught playing one up and one back against the same formation, follow these rules:

>> Players in the back play steadily, mainly crosscourt until they get a short ball that they can use to approach the net. Use the lob over the net man as a variation.

>> Players at the net move up and back in the service box trying to poach or defend against the poach.

Serve to the body or to the middle when you know your partner will try to cross.

If you know your partner will try to poach, serve to the middle of the court or into the body to take the angle away from the returner. This strategy will give your partner the best chance of crossing successfully. Of course, if the opponent has a much weaker side, serve to the weakness.

Server's Partner

Most players blame the server when losing their serve, but ironically, unless the server is a master double faulter, the player at the net is probably just as guilty, if not more. As a server's partner, you have a huge responsibility. Help your team by following these simple "laws":

Be active; cover a large area at the net.

Most net players believe that when their partner is serving their main responsibility is to cover the alley or to serve as cheerleaders for their partner. They crowd their alley to make sure nothing goes by and oversee their partner's performance from that vantage point. No, no, no! Be aggressive at the net; cover as much terrain as you can. Make the middle of the court yours. A good way to think about this is to try to get any ball that your partner would have to hit using his inside volley. For example: backhand volley of a right handed player serving to the deuce court.

Your goal at the net is not to cover the alley but to draw the attention of the opponents and tempt them to hit to the alley by constantly trying to intercept their crosscourt shots.

Always consider three options when your partner serves: stay, cross, and fake. Vary your choices.

The main goal of the server's partner should be to get into the returner's head. You need to keep the adversaries guessing by constantly moving. Every time your partner serves, you need to alternate randomly between the following actions:

Stay: Cover your side of the court.

Cross: Try to intercept the return even if it is on the other side of the court.

Fake: Move early towards the middle of the court to tempt the returner to hit down the line towards the alley. Then you will get back quickly to volley the down the line shot for a winner.

Vary your actions and keep the returner guessing. You will win many points on return mistakes by forcing the opponents to watch you instead of the ball.

Use planned crossings.

By letting your partner know before the point starts that you are planning to cross, you can move aggressively without worrying about the alley. Since your partner knows you will cross, he will cover your side of the court.

Play close to the net if the returner is not lobbing.
The closer you are to the net, the easier it is to cover the net and the easier it is to volley. If the opponents never lob play close to the net and take advantage of all of those high volley opportunities that you will get.

Move in the direction of the serve.
Your starting position should be around the middle of the service box, when your partner is serving. As your partner serves, step in the direction of his serve and split step. This movement will get you in the best position to cover the return.

Focus on the net player diagonally across from you.
You will be in a much better position to defend against a poach if you are watching the net player as your partner returns. You can infer the quality of your partner's return by reading the net player's movements. You will also have more time to defend, since you will be able to prepare for a challenging volley as soon as the opponent starts moving across.

Returner

Getting the return in consistently is the most important goal for the returner. However, there are a few more laws that will increase your effectiveness in this position:

Use all your options during the match: crosscourt, down the line, lob and chip and charge.
Keep the opponents guessing your return. Although you will hit mainly crosscourt returns, use all other options as a change-up. Even hitting differently once or twice a game as a team will keep the opponents on their toes.

Hit the shot after the return between the opponents. After that, the options are: back between the opponents, toward the alley, angle or lob.
Too many times players hit a great return and then miss the second shot because they are trying to hit a winner or are not sure where to hit. Deciding in advance to play the second shot between the opponents is a great way to put pressure on the serving team. Make the opponents hit at least two volleys every point, and they will eventually crack.

I Formation

In this formation the server starts close to the middle of the court just like in singles. The server's partner crouches in the **middle** of the service line at the T. He will move to either side of the court after the serve.

This formation will keep the opponents guessing; serve mainly to the T when using this formation.

The best return against this formation is down the line since it keeps the ball the farthest from both players.

Both Back to Return

Against a very good server, have your partner back up to the baseline with you before you return. This will take some pressure away from you since your return does not have to be great. If you choose to play both back, make sure you keep the return in play, conservatively with a good margin for error. Do not play both back if you are planning to hit an aggressive return.

A well positioned team is difficult to pass.

Drill Library

In this section you will find all the drills in the book plus additional drills that you can use in your training.

Developing Stroke Flexibility (Section 3)

Drills for Beginner and Intermediate Players

Different Heights

Players have to hit the ball at three different heights: low, up to four feet over the net; medium, between five and 11 feet over the net; and high, over 12 feet. At first, the players should focus on constantly keeping the ball at a certain height. After they are comfortable doing this, then they should vary their height in the same rally.

Different Lengths

Players should experience with three lengths: short, inside the service box; medium, just past the service line; and long, close to the baseline. One good progression is to start by trying to keep the ball inside the service box, then moving back and trying to hit the ball as close to the baseline as possible. After a while players should work on rallying letting the ball bounce twice to force them to hit the ball short. Both bounces should land inside the baseline. Finally, players should try to rally hitting very short shots that will bounce three times inside the baseline every time.

Different Speeds

Players should experiment with three different speeds: slow, medium and fast. The ideal speed will be different for each player, but the idea is to stay under control, even with the fast hits. If players are missing too much, they should adjust their swing speed accordingly.

Spin Drills
Introduction to Spin

There are several ways to introduce spin to your players. Here are a few ideas that have worked for me.

Use a Large Light Ball

Using a large ball will allow very young players to safely experiment with spin. By brushing up along the side of the ball or down under it, the player will be able to experience firsthand what it means to spin an object. The size of the ball and its slow flight provide excellent feedback to the players.

Use the Palm of the Hand

Using the palm of the hand of your non-hitting hand to press the ball against the strings provides a great platform for novice players to understand spin. From this position the player can move the racquet up or down, keeping the hand still, and observe the ball's rotation.

Bounce and Spin

A good way to introduce the slice is by having players toss the ball up, let it bounce and then try to make the ball spin by using a chopping motion with their racquet across the bottom of the ball. Once the players are able to make the ball rotate, they can try to keep it in the air without letting it bounce by constantly chopping underneath it.

Use the Net Tape

By pressing the ball against the net tape with the racquet and then brushing up to hit it over, the player can feel the concept of hitting up on the ball to make it rotate forward.

Use the Frame of the Racquet

Instruct the player to hit the ball with the frame of the racquet. For topspin, ask the player to try to hit the incoming shot up to the sky with the upper part of the frame. Then instruct the player to use the same swing but to brush behind the ball as opposed to hitting the ball with the frame. Brushing up can be emphasized by having the player stand very close to the net and hand feeding balls right in front of him. The player on the other side will have to swing up on the ball to avoid hitting the net with his follow though.

For a slice serve, have the player try to hit the ball to the other side of the net with the frame using a service motion, leading with the edge of the racquet. Then ask the player to use the same swing, but brush the side of the ball.

OTHER SPIN DRILLS

Once the players are able to hit the ball with different spins, use the following drills to perfect their control of spin.

Slice

Instruct players to rally hitting only slice. As they improve they can rally trying to keep the ball past the service line, then alternate between shots bouncing before the service line and shots past the service line.

Topspin

Ask players to rally hitting only topspin shots. As they improve, they can alternate hitting one flat shot, one shot with slight topspin and one shot with maximum topspin.

Topspin and Slice

Have players rally alternating one slice and one topspin shot.

Low, High, Very High

With the same racquet head speed, the players rally trying to hit one ball low over the net, one high over the net and one very high over the net. The players will have to hit the ball with incremental amounts of topspin to keep it in the court. Make sure the swing speed remains high and constant.

Long, Middle, Short

Players should rally crosscourt hitting a deep shot, an angle just past the service line, and an angle landing before the service line. Just as in the previous drill, the players will have to hit the shots with incremental amounts of topspin. Make sure the swing speed stays constant.

A complete player with flexible strokes is much easier to coach.

Drills to Develop Stroke Flexibility (Section 4)

Here are some feeding drills, wall drills, collaboration drills and competitive technical drills. These drills are for intermediate to advanced players comfortable hitting with spin.

Feeding Drills

Suggestions

›› Feed every type of ball that a player will encounter during a match and work on the technical skills needed to return the feed effectively (topspin, slice, high, low, fast, slow, deep, short, etc.). Make sure the players can hit all five types of groundstrokes, all five types of volleys, and all the other types of shots mentioned earlier.

›› Force the players to move as if they were in a live ball situation. The movement cycle (split step, adjustment steps and recovery steps) should be part of all drills.

›› Feed randomly after a while, even when working on a specific stroke. Do not feed to the same side at the same speed for too long. As soon as the player starts to get into a groove vary your feeds.

›› Use targets as much as possible. Area targets (example: three-by-three-foot targets) are better than object targets (example: a cone) since the players will experience success more often.

›› Feed as close as possible to the type of balls that the player will experience during a match. Do not make the mistake of feeding advanced players very "easy shots" unless they are making a major change in their technique or working on putting the ball away.

›› Make sure all players on the court are active during these drills. Do not have the players wait in line for too long.

›› Try to include a tactical component into every drill whenever you can. For example:

   ›› Explain to the player how to use his practice shot in match play.

   ›› Use a combination of feeds that mirror what the player will encounter during a point such as: a high lob after a shoulder level mid-court shot or a passing shot after an approach shot.

Off the Bounce

Off the bounce shots with both players standing two feet inside the court.

Shoulder Level

Shoulder level shots with both players stopping the opponent's shot with the racquet, bumping it up, and looking for a shoulder level shot after the bounce.

Dipping shots

Both players try to hit all shots with heavy topspin into the service boxes.

Lifting shots

Both players try to hit deep high heavy topspin shots at each other.

Counting

Players count how many shots they can hit to each other between the service line and the baseline in 20 seconds.

Drills Mixing Different Shot Variations

Basic Drill

Two players are at the baseline hitting different types of shots to each other in different directions (either, crosscourt, down the line, one hits crosscourt one hits down the line, one stands in one corner and hits one shot to the forehand and one to the backhand, rallying alternating forehand and backhand shots, etc.).

Variations: There are many variations you can use. Here are a few examples.

Neutral/Dipping

One player hits neutral shots past the service line, the other player hits dipping shots that land before the service line.

Neutral/Off the Bounce

One player hits neutral shots, the other off the bounce shots.

Dipping/Off the Bounce

One player at the baseline hits dipping shots landing before the service line, the other player hits off the bounce shots while standing just behind the the service line.

Lifting/Shoulder Level

One player hits lifting shots, the opponent hits shoulder level shots.

In and Out

Both players alternate hitting neutral and off the bounce shots by moving in and out of the court after each hit. In other words, both players hit a neutral shot from behind the baseline and step into the court to hit the next shot off the bounce in front of the baseline. After each shot, they move up and back, in and out of the court.

Neutral/Everything

One player hits neutral shots, the other one alternates between neutral shots, off the bounce shots, lifting shots and dipping shots.

Lifting/Shoulder Level and Swing Volleys

One player hits only lifting shots, the opponent alternates between shoulder level shots and swinging volleys.

Dipping and Neutral Alternate

Both players alternate hitting one dipping shot and one neutral shot.

DRILLS WITH TWO PLAYERS AT THE NET

Basic Drill

Two players are at the net hitting different types of volleys to each other in different directions (crosscourt, down the line, one hits crosscourt one hits down the line, one stands in one corner and hits one shot to the forehand and one to the backhand, rallying alternating forehand and backhand shots). As with all rhythm drills, the goal should be consistency and repetition. Have the players count their shots.

Variations:

Close up

Both players are very close to the net hitting quick volleys to each other.

Service Line

Both players are standing at the service line hitting low volleys at each other.

Stretch Volleys

Player A hits volleys moving player B from side to side. Player B hits stretched volleys back to player A.

High Volleys/Defensive Volleys

Player A stands behind the service line and feeds one high ball to player B. Player B hits a high volley aiming at player A's feet. Player A hits a half volley back. Player B volleys back with control, and player A hits another high shot. The process is repeated over and over.

Closing in

Two players start at the baseline and try to move toward the net after each shot controlling the volleys until they get so close to the net that they are able to press the ball between their racquet strings.

DRILLS WITH ONE PLAYER AT THE NET AND THE OTHER IN THE BACK

Basic Drill

Two players are hitting different types of shots to each other in different directions (crosscourt, down the line, one hits crosscourt one hits down the line, one stands in one corner and hits one shot to the forehand and one to the backhand, rallying alternating forehand and backhand shots). One player is at the net and the other one is at the baseline.

Dipping/Low Volleys

Player A is at the net on the service line hitting low volleys or half volleys. Player B is hitting only dipping shots from the baseline.

Lob/Volley

Player A is at the net. Player B at the baseline alternates one lob and one neutral shot.

High Volley/Low Volley

Player A is at the net hitting one high volley and one low volley. Player B at the baseline rallies to make this possible.

Ultimate Variation

Player A is at the net. Player B stands in one corner at the baseline and moves player A in every direction possible, mixing high, low, stretch volleys and lobs.

Low Volley/Half Volley

Player A is at the net. Player B is at the baseline hitting dipping shots aiming at the service line. Player A moves up and back alternating hitting one volley and one half volley.

Defensive lob/Off the Bounce Overhead

One player hits high defensive lobs and the other player hits overheads after they bounce.

Overhead/Lob

One player hits only lobs, the other one only overheads.

Variation:

One player hits only lobs and the other one only backhand overheads.

Players should count to see how many balls in a row they can hit without missing.

Mixed Volleys/Mixed Groundstrokes

One player stands on the service line, the other one at the baseline. The baseline player will alternate hitting one neutral shot, one dipping shot and one lifting shot. The net player returns all shots back with control, practicing low volleys, waist high volleys and high volleys or overheads. Players should count how many balls they can hit in a row without mistakes.

Note: Remember in all these drills the players should either collaborate with each other to achieve a large number of repetitions or use targets to practice hitting to a very specific area. Moreover, all the drills can be played on full court, half court with alleys, half court without alleys, only using forehands, only using backhands or alternating. So, each drill can really be tweaked to generate a myriad of slightly different drills.

Force players to compete using very specific shots.

Competitive Technical Drills

Drills with Two Players Hitting from the Baseline
Drill focusing on one shot variation

Basic Drill

Two players are at the baseline competing with neutral shots (past the service line) using the full court, half a singles court or half a doubles court, crosscourt or down the line. Any mistake or short ball results in a point for the opponent.

Variations:

Off the Bounce

Two players compete using only off the bounce shots with both players standing two feet inside the court.

Neutral with Pressure

Two players compete with neutral shots. The players count the number of shots that land between the baseline and the service line during the rally. The winner of the rally gets all those points.

In the Alley

Two players compete. The alley is the court.

Stop and Hit

Two players compete with shoulder level shots. Both players stop the opponent's shot with the racquet, bump it up and hit shoulder level shots after the bounce.

Advanced players are not allowed to bump the ball into the service boxes.

Dipping Shots

Both players compete hitting all shots with heavy topspin into the service boxes.

Lifting Shots

Both players compete hitting deep, high, heavy topspin shots at each other.

Variation:

If the ball lands before the service line the opponent has to attack it with a shoulder level shot, and the point opens up.

Variation:

The player has to approach the net with the shoulder level shot if the lifting shot lands short.

Neutral Shots by Time

Two players compete against each other to see who can hit more shots between the service line and the baseline in a specific amount of time.

21

Two players rally with each other. One can hit wherever he wants, the other has to try to hit 21 shots between the service line and the baseline. If a shot lands within the service boxes the player must subtract one from his count. For any mistake, a player needs to subtract two.

Topspin/Slice

Two players compete against each other. They have to alternate one topspin and one slice shot.

Only Slice

Two players compete against each other using slice. The game can be played as follows: 1. Allowing the ball to bounce anywhere or 2. Only allowing shots past the service line or 3. Having the players alternate one shot in the service box and one past the service line.

Drills Mixing Different Shot Variations

Basic Drill

Two players compete against each other on half the singles court, half the doubles court or on a full court with different types of shots. The drills can be set up in any direction (crosscourt or down the line).

Variations:

Neutral/Dipping

One player hits neutral shots. The other player hits dipping shots into the service boxes.

Neutral/Off the Bounce

One player hits neutral shots. The other one has to play inside the baseline, hitting off the bounce shots.

Lifting/Shoulder Level

One player hits lifting shots. The other one hits shoulder level shots.

In and Out

Both players alternate hitting neutral and off the bounce shots by moving in and out of the court after each hit. In other words, both players hit a neutral shot from behind the base line and step into the court to hit the next shot off the bounce. After each shot, they move up and back and in and out of the court.

Lifting/Shoulder Level and Swinging Volleys

One player hits only lifting shots. The opponent alternates between shoulder level shots and swinging volleys.

Slice vs. Topspin

One player can only hit slice. The opponent has to hit only topspin.

Again, all these drills can be played only with forehands, only with backhands or using both. During these drills the players could alternate every two points so that both get to hit the different type of shots, or they can play the whole game using the same shot and then play another game switching off. For example, if one is hitting neutral shots, the other might hit dipping shots. They can alternate every two points, or one player can play the whole game hitting neutral shots and then another game hitting dipping shots.

Drills with two Players at the Net

Basic Drill

Two players are at the net competing with different types of volleys in different directions (crosscourt or down the line). As with all competitive technical drills, the goal is to beat the opponent. They play in half the court with or without alleys.

Variations:

Volley Battle

Both players start at the service line and compete hitting quick volleys to each other in half the singles court. Players are not allowed to move forward or backward.

In the Alley

Both players start at the service line and play in the alley either only with forehands or only with backhands. They can play in the whole alley hitting as hard as they want or on half the alley with touch and no bounces allowed.

Mini no Bounces

Two players compete in the service boxes of half the singles court. The ball is not allowed to bounce, and they are not allowed to hit hard.

Mini Serve and Volley

Two players compete in the service boxes of half the singles court. Player A serves underhanded and has to go to the net. The ball is not allowed to bounce on his side. Player B can let the ball bounce. The game is played without a speed limit. The players alternate serving.

Volley Challenge

Two players start at the service line. Both players have to hit and move forward trying to get to the net. One player starts the point underhanded. The point is played out. The game is played on half the court either with or without alleys.

Deep Volleys

Two players are at the net, just behind the service line playing on half a singles court. They cannot step into the service box. They hit volleys trying to hit the ball past the service line. If the ball lands before the service line, the player loses the point.

Forehand Volley in the Alley

Two players start at the service line but in the alley. They are only allowed to hit forehand volleys and the balls are allowed to bounce, but the players are not allowed to move back past the service line. The point is played out. The alley is the court.

DRILLS WITH ONE PLAYER AT THE NET AND THE OTHER IN THE BACK

Basic Drill

Two players are competing hitting different types of shots. One is at the baseline, the other one at the net (crosscourt or down the line). They play on half the court with or without alleys.
Variations:

Lob vs. Overhead

Player A is at the net and cannot let the ball bounce. Player B is at the baseline. The player at the net can only hit overheads. No backhand overheads allowed. The player at the back can only hit lobs.

Lob/Volley

Player A is at the net and cannot let the ball bounce. Player B at the baseline alternates one lob or lifting shot and one neutral or dipping shot.

Dipping Shots/Low Volleys

Player A is at the service line. Player B is at the baseline. Player B hits dipping shots inside the service box. Player A volleys or hits half volleys past the service line.

CONTRAST DRILLS

These are drills in which the alternating use of heavier and lighter objects over-stimulates and under-stimulates a player's muscles to force a faster-than-normal response. For example:

Medicine Ball Throws

Throw a medicine ball six times, as fast as possible, followed by six maximum speed swings. This exercise can be done with groundstrokes or with serves. To improve groundstroke acceleration, use two-handed throws mimicking a forehand or backhand. To improve serve speed, use overhead throws.

Badminton Racquet

Alternating a badminton racquet with a tennis racquet and shadow swinging each six to eight times at maximum speed, followed by six to eight groundstrokes using the same maximum speed swing.

Weighted Racquet

Swing a racquet with a racquet cover or an additional weight at maximum speed six to eight times, swing without it and then swing the same way hitting a ball.

Note: In order for these drills to be effective, all swings and throws need to be executed at **maximum speed.**

RACQUET HEAD SPEED DRILLS

These are drills in which the player learns to swing the racquet head as fast as possible. They usually emphasize forearm and wrist speed. For example:

Ball Against Net

The player stands three feet from the net and tries to hit the ball into the net as fast as possible six to eight times. The swings should be executed with very small backswings at very high speeds.

Fast Feed Drill

The coach stands next to the player and tosses six to eight balls in the air one after the other in fast succession. The player is instructed to swing as fast as possible catching the ball in the air before it hits the ground. The player will be forced to use very fast and compact swings as a consequence of the coach's fast tempo feeds.

Regular Feed Drill

The coach stands on one side of the net and feeds balls. The player stands three feet inside the court and either takes the balls right off the bounce (half volley) or in the air and swings as fast as possible with great amounts of spin.

TACTICAL THEORY DRILLS (SECTION 6)

Same Distance to the Bounce

A good exercise to practice this up and back movement is to rally trying to maintain the same distance between the bounce and the contact point on every shot. This will force the player to constantly adjust forward or backward for each shot. The ideal distance between the bounce and the contact point varies from five to seven feet depending on the individual player's ability and speed of the incoming ball.

Same Rhythm

The same result can be obtained by having the players rally trying to mentally keep a constant rhythm between the bounce and the hit. The player should mentally say "bounce" as the ball bounces and "hit" as he makes contact with the ball. The player should move in such a way as to maintain the same lapsed time between both words. (Example: bounce..hit, bounce..hit, bounce..hit, as opposed to bounce..hit, bounce.......hit, bounce..........................hit, bounce....hit.)

Standard Response Feeding Drill

The coach feeds drop shots, and the player runs them down and hits deep down the line when forced or crosscourt when in control.

Standard Response Situation Drill

Two players are on the court playing singles. The coach feeds drop shots, and one of the players runs them down and hits deep down the line when forced or crosscourt when in control. The point is played out.

Guided Tactical Drill

Two players play singles points. Whoever wins a point with a drop shot gets three points. The player retrieving the drop shot will win three points if he counters the drop shot down the line and one point if he wins the point by countering the drop shot crosscourt.

DOUBLES DRILLS

The same concept can be used with the doubles laws of the battle. Here are a few examples:

Law: Never let the lobs bounce.

Standard Response Feeding Drill

A player starts at the net as if his partner is serving. The coach feeds a deep lob trying to pass him. The player reacts as quickly as possible and tries to hit an overhead. With more advanced players, you can start with the player touching the net. After a while, the coach will vary the feeds, trying to surprise the player at the net with a lob.

Standard Response Situation Drill

Four players take their positions on the court as if starting a doubles point. The coach lobs over one of the players at the net. The player reacts as quickly as possible and tries to hit an overhead. The point is played out. Similarly, players can play the point out, but when one serves, the returner has to lob. If the ball bounces over the opponent's head, the point is over. With advanced players, the net man should start touching the net.

Guided Tactical Drill – Three, Two, One

Points are played out with two players at the net against two in the back. The team at the net starts the point with an underhand feed. The point is played out. Every unforced error counts one point. Every winner counts two points. The team at the net can score three points if they are able to hit an overhead winner. The team at the baseline can win three points if the ball bounces on the other side either in front of the net players or behind them with a good lob. (Once the ball bounces, the point is over.) The game is played until a team reaches 21.

Law: Be active; cover a large area at the net.

Standard Response Feeding Drill

A player is at the net in the server's partner position. The coach feeds from the baseline as if returning a serve. The coach varies the feeds forcing the player to cover any shot crossing the net between the doubles alley and the center of the court (lobs included).

Standard Response Situation Drill

Four players are on the court in doubles formation. One player serves and the coach feeds a return. The player at the net (server's partner) tries to intercept as many feeds as possible. The point is played out.

Guided Tactical Drill

Drill 1

Four players play doubles points. Any point won by poaching counts double.

Drill 2

Four players play doubles points. The server serves and volleys. The server is not allowed to hit any volley with his inside stroke (backhand when serving to the deuce court and forehand when serving to the ad court). The server's partner has to try to intercept any returns towards the middle of the court.

Neutral at the Beginning

Players play points but are not allowed to make a mistake in the first four to six shots. A mistake made during this period should have a negative consequence such as losing more than one point or doing some physical work such as sit-ups.

With advanced players you can make the drill more challenging by giving them a smaller target, such as having them hit the first few shots over the service line.

Points past the Service Line

Players play points on the whole court but are only allowed to hit past the service line. Any ball bouncing in the service boxes is considered a mistake.

Variation:

Players count the shots that land past the service line during the rally. At the end of the point the player who wins the point is awarded the sum of all the shots landing past the service line.

Avoiding the middle

A circle or square is marked in the middle of the court (about six feet in diameter or per side and with the intersection of the service lines as middle). The players play points but lose the point if they play into the marked section.

Attacking the Short Ball

A line is drawn on the court between the service line and the baseline. The distance to the baseline depends on the level of the players. Player A tries to play neutral shots between this line and the baseline. Player B has to play a neutral shot back toward the middle of the court when A's shot lands deep past the line and attack towards either sideline if it lands before the line. The point is played out.

Attacking and Defending

Lifting Shots and Shoulder Level Shots

Players play points using lifting shots. Any player can attack with a shoulder level shot if the ball is short. (The definition of short will depend on the ability of the players.) After that the point opens up.

Variation:

Player A stands inside the court, the opponent, player B, plays a deep lifting shot. Player A has to retreat and play a lifting shot back. Player B will play a shoulder level shot if the ball lands short and a lifting shot crosscourt if it bounces deep.

Variation:

Players play points with the lifting shot until one of them takes the ball in the air with a swinging volley, and the point opens up.

Three Serve Points

Players play points with one extra serve (three serves) with the objective of forcing the opponent to hit a short return. The server tries to finish the point in three shots (including the serve) or will lose the point. The server should practice executing the basic patterns of serving wide and attacking the open court, or serving to the T and attacking either the open court or hitting behind the returner.

Variation:

Same concept except the returner has to return the serve crosscourt or down the middle, which means that if both players are right handed, the return off the backhand side should land on the server's backhand side of the court and vice versa.

One Serve Points

Players play points with one serve. The player returning tries to finish the point in three shots forcing him to play a very aggressive return. If the returner is not able to finish the point in three shots, he loses the point.

Inside Out Forehand Situations

Both players start at the baseline, one starts in the middle and the other one at the singles sideline of the deuce court. The player on the sideline starts the point with a high, easy shot down the line. The other player runs around the backhand and hits an inside out forehand. The player who started the point runs and plays a lifting shot crosscourt with his backhand. If the ball lands deep, the opponent will play another inside out forehand. If the ball lands short, he will play a forehand to the open court. The point is played out.

Variation:

The player who starts the point from the sideline can decide what shot to hit off the inside out forehand. If the inside out forehand gets him into a defensive position, he will play crosscourt; if he can attack the inside out forehand, he will go down the line.

Variation:

The player returning plays a down the line passing shot off the server's first volley. The server angles off the second volley.

Variation:

The first passing shot is hit crosscourt and the volley down the line.

Variation:

The player who returns hits a crosscourt lob off the server's first volley.

First Volley Drill

One player starts at the service line, the other one at the baseline. The player at the baseline starts the point with a low ball at the net player's feet. The net player hits a deep volley and opens up the point. The first volley has to pass the service line. The point is played out. The positioning of the net player during the drill should be emphasized.

Variation:

The baseline player can start the point with a low shot or a lob.

Handling the Drop Shot

Two players start at the baseline. The coach feeds a drop shot to one of the players. The player should run up and hit deep down the line if not in a good position and crosscourt if able to attack. The point is played out.

Variation:

Players rally crosscourt with slice until one of them hits the drop shot, and the point is played out.

Defensive Lob

Two players start at the baseline close to the sideline. One of them feeds a high short ball. The opponent hits an aggressive shoulder level shot crosscourt and approaches the net. The opponent runs the shot down and hits a high defensive lob. The point is played out.

Variation:

The player running down the shot could attempt a passing shot but if he misses, he faces special consequences such as a few kangaroo jumps, sit-ups or pushups.

Variation:

The player running down the shot hits a short, low, backhand slice, forcing the volleyer to hit a low volley, and the point is played out.

Introduce spins early in the development process.

This drill can be performed with many teams. One team is on one side of the court. Those players are the kings of the court and will play against the rest of the teams who line up on the other side of the net. The first team in line plays a point against the kings. If they lose the point, the next team takes its position and challenges the kings. If a team wins two points in a row or hits a winner against the kings, it displaces them and becomes the new team to beat.

MOVEMENT DRILLS (SECTION 8)

GENERAL MOVEMENT

Strike Zone

Players rally, first focusing on their footwork. Once they find a stance that feels comfortable for each stroke, they try to reach this stance every time before they hit the ball. Players should experiment with all strokes.

After they identify a stance that works for them, they will change their focus to the contact point. They will experiment and find a contact point that feels solid, powerful and that allows them to stay balanced throughout the shot.

Ideal Intensity

Players should experiment with different degrees of intensity between hits until they find their ideal level. Intensity is basically movement. Players should bounce on their toes between hits. How much, how high, how fast, etc. is all personal. However, the body needs to remain in motion.

Once players find this ideal level of intensity, they need to make it a habit to work at that intensity level every time they are on the court.

Reach every Ball

Drill 1

Players play singles points using the whole court, including doubles alleys.

Demand proper footwork even when hand feeding.

Drill 2

Players play points, and they are not allowed to stop moving until they touch the ball, even if it is after the second or third bounce or after it has touched the fence. They need to chase the ball even if it bounced outside the lines.

Fight for the Lobs

A player is at the net covering half the court including the doubles alley. The coach or another player moves him around, mixing up his shots. The goal is to get the player at the net out of position and to lob over his head. Every time the player is lobbed or is forced to hit a backhand overhead, he has to do five push-ups.

Expect the Ball to Return

Players play points with a ball in their hand. At any point during the rally, they can choose to put the ball that they are holding in play, even after they just missed a shot. The opponent must be ready to react. **Always!**

React, do not Guess

For the next drill ask the player to start close to the net to limit his reaction time and expose his weakness.

You or another player will feed a ball from the baseline, first tossing it up and then hitting it away from the net player. You should try to mix the feeds, forcing the volleyer to react in different directions. Make sure to include lobs. He will start a few feet from the service line and should start moving towards the net as soon as the coach tosses the ball up. The net player should keep his mind alert and be ready to react to the shot. As the coach starts his swing, the player should split and move in the direction of the shot. If you find that he is not not able to move toward the ball every time, he is either not timing his split correctly or is landing out of balance. Practice this periodically and ask the player to apply it in his matches. You will definitely see a difference once he understands the concept of "Don't guess, just move."

On Court Movement (The Movement Cycle)

Mental and Physical Alertness or Intensity

Players are forced to be on their toes the whole time they are on the court. If they are caught flat footed, they should be reminded about their task by having to sprint to the net and back.

Split step

Split Step Technique

First, let's check your technique. Have the athlete take one step and move into his split step. Check the landing. Is he on the balls of his feet? Is he balanced? Make sure that he is able to maintain his landing position without having to step. If you find that the player is tilting in any direction, have him keep trying until he is able to land perfectly still. In addition, check for a slight knee bend with his weight distributed on the balls of his feet. You should be able to slide a credit card under his heels. Once he is able to do this correctly five times in a row ask him to split step, moving as soon as he lands. Simulate the movement required to hit a ball hit to the forehand side, then to the backhand side and then over the player's head. Check for smoothness. His movement should feel explosive and fluid. Now it is time to try this on the court.

Split Step Timing

Ask the player to rally and say "split" as his opponent's racket starts to move and at the same time execute a split step. He should work on synchronizing the contact of his feet with the ground, with the contact of the opponent's strings and the ball. The player should move in the direction of the hit as soon as he lands. Timing is essential. Splitting too soon or too late will render this procedure useless, and the athlete will find himself late in reacting to the shot.

React, do not Guess

As explained earlier on page 266.

FIRST STEP AND ADJUSTMENT STEPS

Here are a few drills that will improve the first step. Please go through these drills in the order that they are presented since they build on each other.

Get Behind the Ball

The coach stands at the service line with a basket of balls. The player will position himself a foot behind the baseline in the middle of the court, without a racket. The coach will toss a ball up and feed it in any direction. The player should split step as the coach starts to swing and try to position his body right behind the incoming ball so that he ends up catching it with both hands right in front of him. The sooner the player is able to place his body in the desired position, the better. The object of this drill is to teach the player to move his body quickly into a position where he waits for the ball. Start with some easy feeds and make them tougher as the player gets more comfortable with the drill.

First Step

The player starts the same way but is on the baseline with a racket. Start the drill by dividing the court into three equal segments. Use any type of markers to do so. Once the markers are in place the coach will feed wide balls that land outside the markers. This time the player will try to move as quickly as possible to the ideal hitting position, swing at the ball and recover back to the middle. He should be able to move to a position outside the marker before the feed crosses the net. Once in a while, the coach will test by purposely hitting a ball into the net. The player should have already reached the marker by the time the fed ball hits the net. The coach should feed a single ball at the beginning, adding more balls as the player starts feeling more comfortable with the drill.

Try to keep the number of balls fed in groups of six or less. Feeding more balls will prevent the player from giving a 100 percent the whole time.

Catch and Hit

The object of the game is to play a regular set with one player hitting the ball and the other one catching and throwing it. The same rules of a regular tennis match apply except the player with the racket is only allowed one serve. The player catching and throwing has to throw from the same position from which he catches the ball. This game will force the player without the racket to attack the ball with the legs and not with the arms. In essence the player throwing is forced to move a good deal quicker because of the limit in reach that he has without the racket.

Pop it up, Shuffle and Hit

Players rally with each other, but stop their partner's incoming ball and pop it up. They will then use shuffle steps to adjust to the ball to achieve perfect balance and hit it over after it bounces.

RECOVERY

Stopping Momentum

The first exercise is for the player to practice stopping his body momentum as quickly as possible on wide balls. Have him practice without a ball first. The player should start in the middle of the court and run to one sideline pretending to hit a shot. Make sure he finishes his hit facing the net with both feet parallel to the baseline. If he hits open stance this will happen automatically, but if he hits with a closed stance, make sure that he rotates and plants the outside foot to stop his body's momentum. Repeat the shadowing to the other side. Be careful on the backhand side, especially if he hits a one handed backhand. Make sure he rotates after the hit and not in the middle of the stroke. Rotating too early will negatively affect his stroke. Once he feels comfortable doing this, add some side steps to recover back to the middle. Stopping his body and recovering should flow together into one motion.

The next step is trying to do this in a live situation. Feed the player some balls side to side and practice this hitting and stopping while actually hitting balls.

Great movement leads to balanced swings.

STRESS DRILLS

Sets Switching Racquets

Two players play a set. At any time, the coach can call for them to switch racquets with each other. This will force the players to learn to adjust to unexpected situations during competition.

One Serve

Players play a set with just one serve.

This drill will not only help develop a better second serve but will also teach them how to handle the pressure facing a second serve on key points.

Variation:

Two players play a set with one serve. The player who misses the serve or the return loses two points.

Variation:

The player who misses the serve or the return loses the game.

Underhand Serve

Players play a set without serve. The point has to be started underhand but there is no other serving rule. The player can hit anywhere on the court at any speed. However, if the ball does not land on the singles court, the player loses the point.

Approach Set

Two players play a set starting with a short ball as a serve. The opponent approaches the net, and the point is played. You can play this game with regular scoring, or you can add an additional consequence for missing the approach shot or the first passing shot.

Three Points in a Row

You play a set, but can only win a game by winning three points in a row. This will force the players to concentrate on every point and will expose them to many key points every time one of the players wins two points in a row.

The art of coaching is choosing the right drill at the right time.

Consistent Approach/Pass

A set is played, but any missed approach shots or first passing shots count double (the player loses two points). This drill forces the players to concentrate on these two shots, approach and pass, which are very often overplayed. The drill helps players discover their own best way to reduce unforced errors while forcing the opponent.

No Ad at Deuce

Two players play a set with no ad scoring starting at deuce. That means you play one point per game.

Variations:

1) You score the same but start the point with a high defensive lob.
2) You start the point with a lob that has to be taken out of the air with a volley.
3) You start the point with a short ball so that the opponent can attack.

This drill makes every point a key one, so any mistake is costly.

Set at Deuce

A set is played with regular scoring, starting every game at deuce. This format forces the players to face many important points, since every point they lose means almost losing the game.

Geometry of the Court
(Section 6, Tactical Theory)

The geometry of the court is a concept that explains how to cover the court efficiently. Looking at the court from the perspective of court coverage, we know that a key element of footwork is getting back toward the middle immediately after every shot. But where exactly should we recover to?

Understanding the geometry of the court will help us answer this question because the exact middle of the court is not always the ideal position to wait for the next shot.

Guided Tactical Drills
(Section 7, Integrating the Tactical Theory into the Game)

The guided tactical drills are closest in nature to open play and are a key element of the player development process. Just as the situation drills, they are designed to teach the players how to play tactically smart tennis or in other words how to use their weapons in battle. In these drills, the players face different situations on the court that force them to apply the laws of the battle. These drills are more demanding because the player has to analyze a variable situation and decide what the appropriate response is. They are much closer to match play. For example: If you want your players to understand when they are in a position to attack and when they should play neutrally or defensively, you would set up the following drill:

Players play singles points, but have to yell out "yes" or "no" before the opponent's ball crosses the net. "Yes" means they are in a position to attack and will do so. "No" means they are in a defensive or neutral position and will play accordingly.

The goal of these drills is to help players incorporate the laws of the battle into their games.

Laws of the Battle
(Section 6, Tactical Theory)

Tennis, like everything else in life, has a set of rules that make life easier when followed but complicate matters when not. I call this set of rules: the laws of the battle. They describe the ideal response to any situation that a player may encounter on the court, just like a chess manual describing the best move for every position on the board. They are the theory behind the tactical aspect of the game, and the first step towards helping players understand how to use their weapons effectively, or in other words understand where to hit their shots in order to have the best chance of winning the point.

The Lifting Shot

(Section 3, Developing Stroke Flexibility)

The lifting shot is used to hit the ball high over the net with a lot of topspin. A player uses this shot when in a defensive position and out of balance, to change the pace of a rally, or to hit a topspin lob. The shot should be hit with heavy topspin, steeply accelerating the wrist and the forearm. It should clear the net by six to 15 feet depending on the situation.

The Movement Cycle

(Section 8, Movement)

The movement cycle is a series of basic movement patterns that players need to master and repeat over and over to move more effectively on the court.

Each movement cycle starts when the opponent is about to hit the ball and ends after the player has recovered from his shot. So, a player will complete one or more movement cycles during each point depending on how long the point lasts. The following example will illustrate the different components of each movement cycle: Let's visualize a player getting ready to receive a serve. Before the opponent serves, he gets mentally and physically ready to move (component one); as the opponent is about to make contact with the ball the player prepares the body to react in the direction of the incoming shot, by split stepping (component two); then he moves his body in the direction of the ball as soon as possible using an explosive first step and a few adjustment steps (component three), after which he will hit the ball. The last component of the movement cycle is the recovery. After the player hits the ball, he will have to stop his lateral momentum and move back towards the middle of the court as soon as possible to cover the opponent's next shot (component four). So to summarize, the components of the movement cycle are:

1. Mental and Physical Alertness or Intensity
2. Split Step
3. First Step and Adjustment Steps
4. Recovery

Net Rusher

(Section 9, Game Styles)

The net rusher is a player who tries to get to the net as often as possible whether serving or returning.

The Neutral Shot

(Section 3, Developing Stroke Flexibility)

The neutral shot is used to build the point – to plan an attack when a player is not in an ideal position to attack but wants to make sure that the opponent is not able to attack him either.

The neutral shot should be played between one and three feet over the net, deep in the court and with a high degree of consistency. A good way to quantify the speed at which to hit a neutral shot is by setting a goal to hit six to eight shots in a row without missing. Why six to eight shots? Simply because, most points do not last longer than that. If a player hits too hard, he will not be able to hit six to eight shots in a row, and if he is able to hit several more shots in a row it means that he is capable of controlling the ball at higher speeds and therefore should be more aggressive to increase the effectiveness of his game.

The Off the Bounce Shot

(Section 3, Developing Stroke Flexibility)

The off the bounce shot, or half volley, is used in defensive situations when the opponent's ball lands very close to the player so that the player is not able to back up, and when returning a first serve. In both cases the player needs to shorten his backswing and drive through the ball using the opponent's pace. The goal of the shot is to return to a neutral situation in the point.

Pressure Drills

(Section 10, Dealing with Competitive Pressure)

Pressure drills are designed to put the players under stress during practice to test their games and prepare them for competition. There are two types of pressure drills: series drills and stress drills.

Pure Acceleration Exercises

(Section 5, Racquet Acceleration)

These exercises are designed to strengthen the muscles as well as to improve neuromuscular coordination to achieve higher racquet head speeds. Control is absolutely unimportant in these drills. As a matter of fact, these drills will probably be more effective when executed outside the court or against the fence, so that the players can fully concentrate on accelerating without worrying about control.

There are two types of pure acceleration drills: contrast drills and racquet head speed drills.

Racquet Head Speed Drills

(Section 5, Racquet Acceleration)

Drills in which the player learns to swing the racquet head as fast as possible. They usually emphasize forearm and wrist speed.

Relaxation and Swing Development Exercises

(Section 5, Racquet Acceleration)

The goal of this type of exercises is to teach the players to swing effectively using as little effort as possible.

Generally, players will muscle the ball when trying to hit harder instead of letting the racquet head swing faster through the air. To swing at high speeds the player needs to learn to engage only the muscles needed and to relax all other muscles that could slow down the swing. This can only happen if the player is totally relaxed throughout the swing. Any tension will reduce swing speed by engaging muscles unrelated to the action. It is like driving a car with a handbrake on. The car will move, but not as fast or as effortlessly as it should.

Series Drills

(Section 10, Dealing with Competitive Pressure)

Series drills are the best drills to help players get to know their games better. In series drills, players work together to try to complete series of consecutive shots. These shots should mirror typical shot combinations during a point. The goal of these drills is to teach the players how aggressively they can play without making mistakes. They combine the idea of swinging fast and staying under control.

Shoulder Level Shot

(Section 3, Developing Stroke Flexibility)

The shoulder level shot is used to attack from the shoulder level. Technically the preparation should be at shoulder level to allow the player to hit through the ball with little spin and great power. Hit from inside the court off a short, high ball, the final objective of the shot is to hurt the opponent.

Standard Response Drills

(Section 7, Integrating the Tactical Theory into the Game)

The standard response drills are closed end drills in which the player practices the best tactical response to a specific shot over and over. For any given shot, there are normally only a few response options that will give the player the best chance of winning the point. These "correct responses" are what I call "standard responses." For example: If the player is forced off the court with a great shot from the opponent, his best option is to play a high, deep crosscourt shot. This type of shot will give the player the best chance of staying in the point and eventually winning it. In other words, the standard response to a very forcing shot from the opponent is to play a high deep crosscourt shot back.

The goal of these drills is to help players incorporate the laws of the battle into their games.

Standard Response Feeding Drills

(Section 7, Integrating the Tactical Theory into the Game)

These drills involve feeding the ball to the player to have him practice the right response to a given situation over and over. These drills have two stages. In the first stage, the coach will feed the same shot over and over and the player will practice the correct response to that shot. For example: If the goal is to have the player use a deep lifting shot crosscourt every time that he is pulled wide, the coach can feed a wide ball over and over and work on the correct execution of the deep lifting shot. If he wants the player to hit a deep ball down the line in response to a drop shot, he will feed drop shots, and the player will run and hit deep down the line. Simple.

The second stage involves varying the feeds and having the player recognize the situation being targeted and respond accordingly. For example, going back to our first example, if the player has to hit high and crosscourt when pulled out wide, the coach will vary the feeds and look for a high crosscourt shot when the player is forced wide.

Standard Response Situation Drills

(Section 7, Integrating the Tactical Theory into the Game)

Situation drills are basically more sophisticated standard response feeding drills. They are feeding drills, but involve two or four players playing points starting with the situation that is being practiced. In all of these drills the coach or one of his players will feed a ball and force the opponent to repeatedly practice the correct response to a given situation. However, once the player responds to the feed, the point is played out. These types of drills allow the coach to focus on and control more than one tactical response at a time. One player's response to the feed will force his opponent to evaluate and come up with his own response to that shot. For example: If you want your player to start the attack with an inside out forehand when encountering a slow mid-court shot to the backhand, then you would feed this type of shot to him and he would start the point with an inside out forehand. His opponent would hit a crosscourt backhand if the ball is deep and a backhand down the line on a shorter shot. The point is played out.

Stress Drills

(Section 10, Dealing with Competitive Pressure)

Stress drills are exercises designed to teach the players how to compete.

All these drills involve two players competing against each other. To reach our objective it is important to build into the exercise negative consequences for the loser, (for example: some type of physical activity, picking up the balls, buying a sport drink, etc.).

Stroke Flexibility

(Section 3, Developing Stroke Flexibility)

Stroke flexibility is the ability to hit the ball with the desired combination of spin, direction, height, length and speed. In other words, total ball control.

Wall Drills

(Section 3, Developing Stroke Flexibility)

Practicing against the wall is an excellent way to improve technique and develop ball control. One can practice any type of shot against the wall. The key is to be specific. For example: Do not practice backhands, but practice specific types of backhands, such as dipping shots.

Developing High Performance
Tennis Players
ISBN 978-3-944526-01-0

© Copyright 2013, 1st Edition
Neuer Sportverlag, Stuttgart, Germany

Author

Edgar Giffenig

Coordination & Editing

Hendrik Schulze Kalthoff

Martin Frischauf

Design Concept

Pars pro toto Advertising Agency

Nadine Müller

www.parsprototo.com

Layout & Design

Nadine Müller, Tatjana Ziegler

Publisher

Neuer Sportverlag

Siberburgstrasse 112

D-70176 Stuttgart, Germany

Phone +49 (0)711/6 66 14-33

www.neuersportverlag.de

Pictures

TennisGate:

8, 11, 13, 16, 23, 26, 27, 29, 49, 51, 53, 54, 55, 56 middle/right, 57, 58 down, 59, 60 middle/right, 61, 65, 67, 76, 82, 83, 85, 89, 90, 94, 96, 104, 106, 113, 117, 120,121, 127, 131, 132, 135, 140, 143, 145, 146, 149, 159, 170, 173, 189, 192, 195, 197, 199, 202, 206, 209, 211, 215, 216, 220, 227, 238, 245, 269, Cover, Cover small middle, Cover back

Edgar Giffenig:

4, 6, 15, 19, 21, 22, 24, 30, 31, 35, 37, 38, 41, 45, 52, 56 left, 58 up, 60 left, 63, 68, 70, 78, 81, 87, 91, 93, 101, 102, 107, 109, 115, 119, 123, 125, 128, 137, 138, 152, 154, 157, 164, 167, 168, 175, 176, 180, 183, 184, 205, 212, 253, 259, 265, 273, Cover small left/right, Cover Portrait EG

NEUER SPORTVERLAG

My-Pocket-Coach E-Books

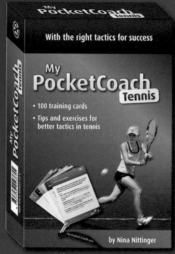

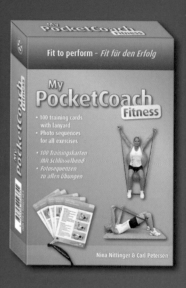

My-Pocket-Coach Psyched-up
E-Book ISBN 978-3-938023-73-0
E-Book USD 12,99 (EUR 9,99)

My-Pocket-Coach Tennis
E-Book ISBN 978-3-938023-74-7
E-Book USD 12,99 (EUR 9,99)

My-Pocket-Coach Fitness
E-Book ISBN 978-3-938023-78-5
E-Book each USD 12,99 (EUR 9,99)
ISBN 978-3-938023-76-1
Printed Training Cards EUR 29,90

My-Pocket-Coach is the ultimate tool for athletes and trainers to improve mental, physical and tactical strengths in training and competition. Mental strength, fitness and tactical finesse play an enormously important role in optimizing or maintaining sporting capabilities.

My-Pocket-Coach Psyched-up lets athletes from all sports quickly acquire important awareness about psychological aspects. Practical exercises help to build up specific mental strengths. My-

Pocket-Coach always gives you the right tips for those decisive moments, whether in training or in competition.

My-Pocket-Coach Tennis is the effective advice for every tennis player, as it provides solutions to help succeed in difficult situations. My-Pocket-Coach Tennis gives ambitious players tactical match tips that help lead to victory. A player that wants to win a match needs to understand how to beat their opponent.

Neuer Sportverlag | Silberburgstr. 112 | DE-70176 Stuttgart | Germany | info@neuersportverlag.de | www.neuersportverlag.de